CW01510824

A Pub Landlord's Guide to the Cotswolds

A Pub Landlord's Guide to the Cotswolds

A Pub Landlord's Guide to the Cotswolds

Warren Turner

A Pub Landlord's Guide to the Cotswolds

Published by Drunken Sailor Events Ltd

ISBN: 978-1-0369-0891-1

DEDICATION

This book is dedicated to my wonderful husband, Norman, and our two rescue dogs, Beaker and Bunsen. Without the three of them, life in the Cotswolds would be so much more boring. More relaxed perhaps. No, just more boring.

Contents

ACKNOWLEDGMENTS

Writing this guide has mostly been a joyful experience. As with any project like this, there were many people who made the task easier, who tolerated my daft questions or who offered skills that I lack, to ensure the book could be completed. Chief among them is my husband and business partner, Norman Liu, who has better IT skills than even he will admit to, and an eye for design. Norman, thanks for the cover design, drawing the Cotswold map and for listening to me (mostly impatiently) endlessly testing out passages of text on you. You have been very patient with me – though that is what you signed up for!

Thank you to all the lovely staff and guests of the Horse and Groom Inn, Upper Oddington. I left an early version of the text of the book just lying about the pub, loosely bound, for staff and guests to pick up, read and leave comments on. It's still around somewhere and is now very well thumbed and falling apart. To everyone who encouraged, bribed or blackmailed people to read this early version, I owe you a debt of gratitude. The feedback and comments gained both encouraged me to complete the job and helped me to improve the book's content and layout.

Finally, to my parents, Jane and Derek and my wonderful extended family, thank you for being so encouraging and supportive. I know you all think we lost what few marbles we ever had when we decided to buy the pub. You were nevertheless a great support when we did and continue to drink us dry whenever you come to visit, which can never be often enough!

PREFACE: HOW TO USE THIS GUIDE

First, don't take any of it too seriously or literally! Over the years of owning the pub and hosting thousands of guests from all over the globe, I have provided endless advice -whether wanted or not – on where to go, what to see, and what to do when visiting the Cotswolds. I've also heard back from guests about their views, opinions and impressions of the area and found much of what people have to say about the Cotswolds both amusing and bemusing. I've also discovered that no question from visitors to the area is really ever too stupid. These often amuse me too. Take for example the lady who asked, "are the locals here all farmers?" or the loud brash tourist who asked, "why are the roads here so narrow? Didn' t they think of the width of cars when building them?"

I've even been asked on several occasions to order a guest an Uber or whether Deliveroo will deliver takeaway food to the pub (when our kitchen has been closed). My advice for anyone visiting the Cotswolds is to suspend all your normal expectations. Assume nothing will be open and expect everything to close early. That way, you won't be disappointed when standing outside somewhere that closed an hour ago in the pouring rain. Anyone in these parts who is still awake after 9pm is viewed with deep suspicion!

If you do need a taxi anywhere at any time, just remember to organize it about six months in advance and don't depend too much on it turning up!

This guide has been written with all these bonkers things in mind and, most probably, been written when I've been a bit overwhelmed and influenced by the heady fumes of beer, wine and spirits in the pub. It is, therefore, mostly a mix of interesting facts about Cotswolds places mixed in with a muddle of utter nonsense and general frivolty. The game here, really, is for you to filter out the useful stuff. Please don't be offended by anything written in the book, it's meant to be a bit of fun.

If you are the owner of one of the places in the guide and feel upset or offended by anything I have written or spot a factual inaccuracy, please accept my apology and let me know. Then have a stiff drink and a bit of a lie down. You'll soon get over it.

Also, don't rely too much on contact details, opening hours etc. for places listed. These were all correct at the time of publication but are, clearly, not in my control (regrettably!).

I hope the guide serves as a fun introduction to this wonderful part of England and that it encourages readers to visit some of these ridiculous places.

In particular, please visit the Horse & Groom Inn at Upper Oddington where you can be sure of a warm welcome, a perfectly conditioned cask ale and a hearty meal. If you're lucky, I might even get to pull you a pint!

Warren Turner, 2025.

Horse and Groom Inn, Upper Oddington, GL56 0XH.
www.horseandgroomcotswolds.co.uk. T: +44(0)1451 830584.

Local Area Map

The Cotswolds

1 STOW ON THE WOLD

Stow-on-the-Wold is a Cotswold's town, a bit like if a picture postcard and a jigsaw puzzle had a baby. It's been around since forever—like, pre-history days. But back then, it probably wasn't called Stow-on-the-Wold, because no one had invented the name yet. They were too busy doing things like inventing fire and trying not to get eaten by wolves. Stow is a place where there are always people wearing tweed caps, wellies and no doubt arguing passionately about chutney.

Now, Stow-on-the-Wold is famous for its market square, which is exactly what it says: a square, where a market used to be, and still sort of is, but with more artisanal bread, ceramic napkin rings and fewer sheep. Back in the olden days—medieval times, when everything was a bit dirty, and people thought taking baths was a bit extreme—Stow was a bustling market town. They'd have huge fairs where people traded wool, because apparently wool was the Bitcoin of the 14th century.

And then there was a big battle here in the English Civil War, in 1646. Picture it: loads of blokes in uncomfortable clothes, waving swords about and shouting things like "For King!" or "For Parliament!"—probably without knowing what they were really fighting for, like most people in a heated Facebook debate. The Royalists got properly trounced here, which means they lost, in a posh way. But don't feel too bad for them—they'd picked the wrong side, and history loves winners.

Stow's also famous for its little streets, or "alleyways," which in medieval times were known as "those places where the pickpockets hang out." But now, they're just charming places to buy overpriced fudge or candles that smell like fresh laundry. There's this famous door at St. Edward's Church that looks like something out of 'Lord of the Rings', which is funny because Stow is mostly known for looking ancient and sleepy, but actually it's not even as old as some Hollywood movies. But it does look lovely on Instagram.

And today, it's a perfect example of what Americans think all of Britain looks like: quaint, cobbled, and impossibly old. Which is fair, because it sort of is. Stow-on-the-Wold: the kind of place where time stood still, or at least, took a long nap.

2 BOURTON ON THE WATER

Bourton-on-the-Water is known as the "Venice of the Cotswolds," which makes it sound incredibly glamorous, like a place where people might ride about in gondolas while licking on a Cornetto or sipping Limoncello. But instead of gondolas, they've got little stone bridges, and instead of Cornettoes or Limoncello, there's more scone and tea rooms than you can shake a farm-fresh ice cream at. It's also got a river, the Windrush, which sounds quite poetic, like the sort of place where Wordsworth might have gone to write a poem about how miserable the weather is.

The river isn't very deep, though—more of a puddle, really. You could probably walk across it, and lots of people do, especially children and dogs, who somehow never seem to mind getting their socks wet. It's shallow enough that if you fell in, you'd just feel silly rather than endangered. But that's part of Bourton's charm: it's a place where even the dangers are polite.

Now, historically speaking, Bourton has been here for a while— ages, in fact. Probably since Roman times, when people loved building roads and naming things in Latin. But Romans aren't around anymore, and now it's all about tourists wandering around wondering if they can justify spending £9 on some fudge in the gift shop.

Bourton-on-the-Water is home to some truly remarkable attractions, like the Model Village, which is a tiny version of Bourton itself. That's right: it's a village with a model of itself inside it, which means you could technically go and look at a miniature version of yourself looking at a miniature version of the village, like some sort of low-budget *Inception*. It used to have a lovely Model Railway Exhibition too, but those little trains have been shunted into the sidings somewhere to make space for another tea and ice cream shop. Just how many tea and ice cream shops can one village need? Obviously quite a lot. No danger of any tea or ice cream dependent diabetics becoming at risk of collapse here!

And of course, there's Birdland—like Disneyland, but for people who think birds are more entertaining than roller coasters. It's got flamingos and penguins, because nothing says "Cotswolds" like an exotic flightless bird that probably wishes it was somewhere a bit warmer.

Bourton-on-the-Water is one of those places that's quaint, but with a side of "please keep off the grass." It's the kind of place where people come to get a slice of what they think England looked like a hundred years ago—pretty, a bit slow, and with an awful lot of ducks, tea, ice cream and an endless stream of tourists looking for somewhere to park.

3 BROADWAY

Broadway, Worcestershire, not to be confused with Broadway, New York—which has theatres, musicals, and people shouting at each other in traffic—this Broadway is all about charm, tea shops, and a lot of Cotswold stone. It's called the "Jewel of the Cotswolds," which is a bit of a stretch because if you tried to wear it like a jewel, it would be heavy, and your neck would hurt, and people would look at you funny. But it's very pretty, in that way that makes you think, "Yes, this is what England would look like if it was made by a set designer with a fetish for old stones."

The history of Broadway goes back ages, even before it became a magnet for tourists with cameras and too many layers of clothing. It's got a High Street that's not like the ones in big cities where you've got loads of shops selling trainers or American candy. This High Street is full of old coaching inns, antique shops, and places that sell more types of chutney than you ever thought existed. It's all very picturesque, like a jigsaw puzzle that's slightly too difficult for a lazy Sunday afternoon.

Broadway Tower is the main attraction here. It's a bit like the Eiffel Tower, but made of stone, and much shorter, and less French. It's on top of a hill, so you can go up and have a look around and think, "Yes, this is definitely a view." Apparently, on a clear day, you can see up to 16 counties from the top, which sounds impressive, but let's be honest—you'd have to be a geography teacher to actually identify all of them.

And in the 19th century, Broadway was a sort of hangout for artists and writers—people like William Morris, who was very into wallpaper and socialism. It became a bit of an artists' colony, which is basically like a normal colony, but with more easels and fewer ships. They probably spent their time looking at the hills and thinking deep thoughts like, "What if I painted that tree... but slightly greener?"

Today, Broadway is the kind of place where you can have a cream tea at 3 pm and then have a walk and not do much else. It's got a lot of "atmosphere," which is what people say when a place is too nice to have any actual fun in. But that's its charm. You go there to feel like you've stepped back in time—back to when things were slower, and people genuinely cared about how many types of jam they could buy in one village. Broadway, Worcestershire: it's not quite a musical, but it's a nice place to hum quietly to yourself while you walk around looking for

11

somewhere to have a burger.

4 BROADWAY TOWER

Broadway Tower? Oh, that's like one of those pointless buildings that exist for absolutely no reason, a bit like the Tate Modern Gallery in London, or the Royal Opera House, but somehow people love it. It's basically a big tower plonked on top of a hill in the Cotswolds. The Victorians built it, because they looked at a perfectly good hill and thought, "You know what this needs? A tower no one can live in or use." Probably also because in the days before Netflix there wasn't much else to do in their spare time.

Apparently, it was designed to look like a fairytale castle, but it's more like something you'd build out of cardboard boxes in your garden as a kid. If you stand on top of it, you get a great view, which is mostly just of fields and sheep, which, to be honest, are pretty much everywhere in England. So, why bother going up a tower?

People say it was used as a signal tower back in the day, which is basically like the Victorian version of sending a text message, but with more smoke and fewer emojis. These days, it's a popular tourist spot, because humans love climbing things, even if the reward at the top is just more sky.

In summary, it's a tower. It's broad. And it's a great place to look at other things that are not towers. Perfect for anyone who's ever thought, "I love the countryside, but what if I could be slightly higher while looking at it?"

Broadway Tower: Broadway, Worcestershire, WR12 7LB. www.broadwaytower.co.uk. T; +44 (0)1386 852390

5 CHIPPING NORTON

Chipping Norton, or "Chippy" as the locals call it, which sounds like a place where you might go for some fish and chips but it's really just a town with a lot of Cotswold charm. The name "Chipping" comes from an old English word meaning "market," which is appropriate because it's the kind of place where people used to trade things like wool and probably gossip about whose sheep were the fluffiest. Back then, trading wool was like the original online shopping, but slower and with more sheep-related drama.

It's been around since at least the Middle Ages, which means it's really old. And you can tell, because everything there is made of that honey-coloured Cotswold stone that's so pretty, you almost don't mind that it crumbles a bit when it rains. The town's got a grand church, St. Mary's, which is what they used to build instead of coffee shops. If you wanted to sit quietly and think about the meaning of life, you had to go to a church and not a Starbucks.

In the Industrial Revolution, they built a big mill here, Bliss Mill, where they made wool and made sure people didn't have to freeze during winter. But now it's been turned into posh flats for people who prefer to live in an old factory than a yellow-stoned cottage. It's what happens when you take a town that was once all about hard work and turn it into somewhere people go to escape the hustle and bustle of places like London.

Speaking of London, Chipping Norton is famous for being the home of the "Chipping Norton set," which is basically a group of posh people and celebrities who moved here because they like pretending they live a quaint, rural lifestyle without having to give up all their fancy things. You know, like going to the farmer's market and buying organic carrots while secretly wishing they were in a Michelin-starred restaurant. Don't be disappointed if you meet some of the Chipping Norton Set and find that they are not at all fixed in jelly. The 'set' bit is just that they seem to form part of a group of like-minded people, some of whom went to a posh University and liked to make a living from phone tapping, loathing the EU and pretending to be farmers or pub landlords, sort of like a rogue train set.

It's got the usual Cotswold features: antique shops, tea rooms, and a pub on every corner, all of which look like they could be in a period drama where nothing really happens, except for a misunderstanding about who's invited to the church fete. But it's also got a bit of edge, like it's a town that thinks, "Yes, I'm quaint, but I can still have opinions about the economy."

Chipping Norton is the kind of place where you are likely to see a tractor and a Range Rover in the same traffic jam. It's a town that's stuck somewhere between the past and the present, where people still talk about the weather but also know what a flat white is. Chipping Norton: it's old, it's new, and it's very, very Chippy.

6 SEZINCOTE HOUSE AND GARDENS

Sezincote House and Gardens? Right, so this is a big house in the middle of the Cotswolds that looks like it should be in India, but somehow, it's not. It's like someone said, "What if we built the Taj Mahal... but in Gloucestershire?" And then everyone just nodded and carried on with it like that was a completely normal idea.

The house itself is a mix of Mughal and Regency architecture, which is just a fancy way of saying, "We took bits from all over the place and glued them together." It's got a massive dome, minarets, and even elephants. Not real elephants, of course—because that would be ridiculous—but stone ones, which is slightly less ridiculous but still a bit weird when you remember you're in the English countryside. Imagine a big, fancy house deciding to dress up as another big, fancy house for Halloween. That's basically Sezincote.

Apparently, this place inspired the Brighton Pavilion, which is that other famous building that also looks like it doesn't belong in Britain. So, if you like houses that make you go, "Wait, where am I?" Sezincote's the place for you.

The gardens are lush, exotic, and basically a lesson in how to make things grow in a climate that doesn't really want them to. You wander around and half expect a peacock to walk out and start demanding attention, which wouldn't be out of place, really. There's a huge water feature that looks like something out of an old painting—because rich people love nothing more than water that doesn't do anything except look pretty.

In conclusion, Sezincote is the house equivalent of someone who's travelled the world, picked up a bunch of souvenirs, and then said, "I'm going to wear them all at once." It's impressive, confusing, and a bit bonkers all at the same time—just like the Cotswolds, really.

Sezincote House and Gardens: Moreton in Marsh, Gloucestershire, GL56 9AW. www.sezincote.co.uk.

7 BURFORD

Burford. Now, that's a name that just *sounds* like it should be in the Cotswolds, doesn't it? It's got all the classic Cotswold ingredients: old buildings, a river, and more antique shops than you can shake a vintage walking stick at. It's sometimes called "the gateway to the Cotswolds," which makes it sound a bit like the entrance to a magical kingdom. But instead of talking animals or a wizard, you just get a High Street with lots of people looking for parking or queuing for a macchiato.

Burford has been around for a long time—so long, in fact, that even the Romans probably thought, "Wow, this place has been here a while." It's full of those classic, wonky, honey-coloured houses that make you think, "Ah yes, this is what England should look like." Even the pubs here look like they've been sitting in the same spot since King Henry VIII was around, which they probably have. Burford's got an old church, St. John the Baptist, that's been around since the 12th century. Back then, they didn't have much in the way of entertainment, so building a massive church was pretty much the medieval equivalent of binge-watching a TV series.

One thing Burford is famous for is its steep High Street. You can't miss it because if you walk down it, you might start wondering whether you should have invested in a better pair of shoes. It's lined with shops selling things you didn't even know you needed, like antique egg cups, brushes and posh dog biscuits. It's also got lots of tearooms, because in Burford, sitting down with a pot of tea and a lardy cake is practically a local sport. And if you fancy something stronger, there's plenty of pubs where you can sip a pint and pretend you're in a country costume drama.

Back in the old days, Burford was big on the wool trade, which was basically the 14th-century version of being into tech stocks. All those sheep made the town rich, which is why they could afford to build all those fancy houses. And the river that runs through it, the Windrush, isn't just a pretty feature; it used to be a sort of medieval motorway, which is how they got all those woolly riches from one place to another. Now, it's mainly there so people can take nice photos and kids can try to fall into it.

There's a bit of history in Burford too, like the time in the 1600s when some rebellious soldiers, called the Levellers, got locked up in the church and then shot in the churchyard. Because back then, when people disagreed, they didn't just write a stern letter; they did it with muskets. It's the sort of historical titbit that makes you think, "Well, at least today's arguments mostly stay on social media."

Burford today is a bit of a tourist hotspot, which means you'll find a lot of people in sensible shoes looking at old buildings and saying, "Isn't it charming?" And it is charming—properly charming, like a town that could be in a jigsaw puzzle or a TV show about detectives with unusual hobbies. Burford: it's ancient, it's steep, and it's about as Cotswolds as you can get without turning into a sheep

8 DAYLESFORD ORGANIC FARM SHOP

Daylesford. Now, this place is famous for being a farm shop, but it's not just any old farm shop. It's like the *Rolls-Royce* of farm shops, except instead of selling cars, it sells organic hummus and very pampered carrots. It's in the Cotswolds, which means everything is automatically posh, a bit entitled and made of that honey-coloured stone that looks great on Instagram. And even though it's technically a farm, it's probably the only farm where the mud is artisanal, and the cows have Pilates classes. The hedges are all cut to look the same and make the whole area look and feel more like Disney World than Disney ever managed to achieve at their Parisian theme park.

The thing about Daylesford is that it's all about organic, which means it's like normal food, but you pay more for it because it had a nicer life than you. You can get everything from vegetables that look like they came straight out of a food magazine to candles that smell like a summer meadow but cost more than a night in a Marriott. It's the kind of place where you'd buy an avocado, but it would come with a backstory about how it was nurtured on a south-facing Mexican hillside while listening to Mariachi music played by ginger nuns before being shipped to the Cotswolds in the royal suite of the Queen Mary 2.

And Daylesford isn't just a shop; it's got a whole lifestyle vibe. They've got a spa, because apparently shopping for organic veg is stressful enough that you need to unwind afterwards with an herbal wrap. And then there's the cookery school, where you can learn how to make all sorts of fancy dishes using ingredients that sound like they were named by a poet. I bet they teach you how to roast a parsnip in a way that makes it taste like hope.

It's the brainchild of an absurdly rich person who decided that food should be better, and that people should spend a lot more money on it. So, they made this place where even the chickens probably have their own wellness plans. The whole thing is like a theme park for people who love organic living, but with fewer rollercoasters and more sourdough starters.

People don't just go to Daylesford to buy food—they go to be seen buying food. You can spot them with their wicker baskets looking like they're in a commercial for "the simple life" but wearing a cashmere sweater that costs more than a second-hand car. It's the kind of place where you might bump into a celebrity pretending they're just a normal person picking out Kohl Rabi.

Many won't even think about a visit to Daylesford unless they are able to arrive in a Land Rover Defender, a Range Rover or a big posh car. Hoards will be wearing tweed (even if it's just a tweed cap or knickers) and green wellies (preferably Hunter, or if a bit posh, Le Chameau) that have never been anywhere near mud or anything even slightly moist. The car park here is like a country 4 x 4 showroom full of tweed & wellies-clad city folk who wouldn't know a muddy field if they parachuted into one from their helicopters. They are the 'clean welly' brigade, where wellington boots are fashion accessories not wet-weather utility items.

Daylesford is basically what happens when you take the idea of a farm, turn it up to eleven, and add a lot of hyphens. It's not just a shop; it's a way of life—specifically, a way of life that involves paying five pounds for a loaf of bread. It's the sort of place that makes you think, "I should eat more kale," even if you have no idea what kale actually does. Daylesford: it's a farm shop, but with a splash of *je ne sais quoi* and a lot of quinoa. They also have some fancy-pant pubs in the area where they took some lovely traditional local 16th century country pubs, took out all the lovely original oldness and made them conform to an organic Farrow and Ball style impression of old but with more drum and bass music, year-round open fires and the occasional Beckham.

Daylesford Organic Farm Shop: Daylesford, Near Kingham, Cotswolds, GL56 0YG. www.daylesford.com. T: +44 (0)1608 731700.

9 MORETON IN MARSH

Sounds like the kind of place where you might get a bit damp, doesn't it? Like it's just waiting for you to accidentally step in a puddle. But actually, it's not really that marshy at all. It's just a town in the Cotswolds with a name that's stuck with it since medieval times, probably because back then people didn't have Google Maps and got lost in bogs more often. These days, it's more about cosy tea rooms than soggy socks.

It's been around for centuries, which is a long time, even by Cotswolds standards, where they think anything built after 1700 is "modern." Moreton-in-Marsh started as a coaching town, which means it was like the 18th-century version of a motorway service station, except instead of a Costa Coffee and a dodgy burger van, you had pubs, inns, and horses that needed a rest. People would stop here on their way to London or Birmingham, back when those places were much more exciting than Moreton. Not that Moreton's boring, mind you, but it's more about admiring tea shops than high-speed chases.

The town's big claim to fame is its Tuesday market, which has been going since 1227. That's right, they've been flogging stuff here for nearly 800 years. It's a proper market too, with stalls selling everything from cheese to socks to those little wind-up toys that no one really needs. It's like a medieval Amazon but without the Prime delivery. If you're looking for a cabbage, a woolly hat, or a local painting of a sheep, this is the place.

And then there's the high street, lined with those lovely Cotswold stone buildings that make everything look like it's been dusted with sepia tone. There's the White Hart Royal Hotel, where King Charles I supposedly stayed once, because back then, kings didn't have much choice when it came to accommodation, and they had to settle for wherever had a decent ale and a bed that didn't smell too much like a horse.

Moreton-in-Marsh is also home to Batsford Arboretum, which is basically a fancy word for a really big garden with loads of trees. It's the kind of place where you go to look at leaves and pretend you know the difference between a maple and a sycamore. And there's also the Cotswold Falconry Centre, where you can watch birds of prey doing their thing, which is mainly swooping and looking at you like they think they're better than you.

So, Moreton-in-Marsh is a bit of everything: a market town, a historic pitstop, and a place where you can watch owls fly about and feel a bit closer to nature—without actually having to camp or get mud on your shoes. It's got all the charm you'd expect from the Cotswolds, but with the added bonus of having a train station, so you can escape back to modern life whenever you feel like it. Moreton-in-Marsh: it's not marshy, and it's got tea shops, a great chippy and a caravan site.

10 DIDDLY SQUAT FARM SHOP

Diddly Squat Farm Shop. Now, that's a name that tells you everything and nothing at the same time. It's like calling something "Barely There Café" or "Almost Good Hotel." But actually, it's a farm shop in the Cotswolds that's somehow become as famous as a Hollywood star, all thanks to Jeremy Clarkson, a man known for driving cars very fast and saying things that make people put their heads in their hands.

The shop sits on Clarkson's farm, which is called Diddly Squat because, according to Jeremy, that's how much he knew about farming when he started. And honestly, that's how much most people know about farming too—except maybe farmers. It's in the middle of beautiful Cotswold countryside, surrounded by fields, hills, and probably a lot of confused sheep wondering why there's suddenly a queue of tourists outside.

Now, Diddly Squat Farm Shop is not your average farm shop. You won't just find potatoes and honey—though there is that. It's full of things like "Cow Juice," which is milk, and "Bee Juice," which is honey. Apparently, if you put the word "juice" after anything, it makes it funnier. It's all very rustic and authentic, which is what people say when they mean that things are more expensive than they should be but come with a charming backstory.

The shop itself is a tiny wooden shed, which is probably what makes it feel like such a novelty. It's like a little slice of countryside life, but with a side order of sarcasm. You can buy things like farm-fresh eggs, locally grown vegetables, and bread that's so crusty, you need a small hammer to get into it. There's also Clarkson's own-brand Hawkstone beer and cider, because apparently farming wasn't enough, and he thought, "Why not make something that can get people a bit tipsy too?"

But it's not just about the produce. It's about the experience, which is what businesses say when they want you to pay extra for something you could probably get cheaper somewhere else. People flock here to see the shop, take selfies in front of a sign that says "Opening Times: Whenever We Feel Like It," and maybe catch a glimpse of Clarkson himself, shouting at a tractor or looking confused by a sheep. The whole thing feels a bit like a theme park for people who like to think they understand farming after watching a few episodes of *Clarkson's Farm.*

Of course, being a farm shop run by a man who's famously grumpy, it's had its share of controversy—like traffic jams on quiet country roads and complaints from locals who are used to things being a bit less chaotic and a lot less... Clarksony. But that's all part of the charm, isn't it? A farm shop that's a little bit chaotic, a little bit cheeky, and probably a bit overpriced—but you don't mind, because it makes you feel like you're in on the joke.

So, Diddly Squat Farm Shop: it's not about how much you actually buy—it's about the feeling that you've been part of something unique, even if that something is just a shed in a field with a bloke from the telly selling jam.

Diddly Squat Farm Shop: 5-12 Chipping Norton Rd, Chipping Norton, Oxon, OX7 3PE. www.diddlysquatfarmshop.com.

11 CHIPPING CAMPDEN

If you're looking for a place that's so picturesque it could
practically be a screensaver, this is it. It's like the Cotswolds
decided to really show off and put all its prettiest bits in one
place. The name sounds a bit fancy too, doesn't it? "Chipping" is
an old English word for market, because back in medieval times,
people liked to trade things like wool, gossip, and probably make
the occasional complaint about the weather. It's a bit like eBay,
but with more sheep and fewer delivery options.

The High Street in Chipping Campden is famous for its old buildings made from that classic Cotswold stone—like the town decided to go for a single aesthetic and really commit to it. Walking down the street is like stepping into the past, except you're surrounded by modern things like Wi-Fi and people who say "artisan" a lot. They've got a market hall right in the middle, which is basically an ancient shelter for stalls. It was built in the 1600s to protect traders from the rain, because even then, the British weather had a reputation for being a bit soggy.

Now, back in the day, Chipping Campden was a big deal in the wool trade. It was one of those "wool towns," which sounds like a theme park but is actually just a place where they made a lot of money from sheep. You can still see the evidence in all those grand houses built by wool merchants who wanted to show off just how well they were doing. It's like they were saying, "Look at me, I've got a fancy house and a flock of very successful sheep."

The town's also famous for the Arts and Crafts Movement. That's when, in the 20th century, a bunch of people got together and decided they'd had enough of factories and mass-produced stuff. They wanted to make things by hand, like pottery and furniture—basically Etsy before the internet was a thing. They all came to Chipping Campden to work in little workshops, surrounded by rolling hills and feeling superior about their homemade candlesticks.

Today, Chipping Campden is the kind of place where people go to feel like they've stepped back in time, except with the added bonus of modern conveniences like coffee shops that serve lattes with patterns in the foam. It's full of boutique shops, art galleries, and places where you can buy a handmade scarf that's just itchy enough to remind you it's "authentic." And there's lots of visitors wandering around in sensible shoes, stopping every few feet to take a photo of a doorway or a flowerpot.

You've got to see the Cotswold Way, a long-distance walking path that starts in Chipping Campden. It's for people who think the best way to spend a holiday is by walking so far you end up wondering if your feet will ever forgive you. But the views are worth it, they say, because you can see miles and miles of rolling hills that all look exactly like the cover of a guidebook about the English countryside.

So, Chipping Campden: it's pretty, it's historic, and it's got more charm than a Christmas advert. It's the kind of place that makes you want to buy a woolly jumper, learn about medieval architecture, and maybe try to appreciate the difference between an Arts and Crafts chair and a regular one—even if you'll never actually sit on it. It's like stepping into the past, except with more cake shops and people trying to find the perfect angle for a selfie.

12 STRATFORD UPON AVON

Not strictly speaking a Cotswold town, but near enough to be a favoured neighbour! Stratford upon Avon. That's a town name that really likes to let you know where it is, doesn't it? It's in Stratford, and it's on the Avon, which is a river. But it's not just any old river, it's *the* river, because if you're in England and your town's got a river, it's probably called the Avon. They just didn't get very creative with river names back then.

But the real reason everyone's heard of Stratford-upon-Avon is William Shakespeare, the bloke who wrote all those plays that people pretend to like but secretly find a bit confusing. He was born here, died here, and in between, he wrote a bunch of stuff about people falling in love, stabbing each other, and saying "wherefore" a lot. So now, the whole town is like one giant Shakespeare theme park, but without the roller coasters—unless you count the emotional roller coaster of trying to understand *Hamlet*.

Stratford-upon-Avon has got everything you'd expect from a place that's built its entire brand around a long-dead playwright. You've got Shakespeare's Birthplace, which is a little house where he was born in 1564. It's like a medieval time capsule, except instead of being buried underground, it's got a gift shop and a bunch of tourists taking selfies outside. And there's Anne Hathaway's Cottage, which is where Shakespeare's wife lived, not the actress. It's got a thatched roof, loads of flowers, and it looks like the sort of place where a fairy tale character would bake pies.

The town's got the Royal Shakespeare Company too, which is a theatre group dedicated to making sure people keep reading Shakespeare, even if they'd rather be watching something with fewer rhyming couplets. You can go to the theatre here and see actors being all serious and dramatic while dressed in ruffs and doublets, which is like a medieval version of a tuxedo but more uncomfortable.

Stratford's got a river, as we've established, and you can take a boat trip on it if you like the idea of floating past weeping willows while a guide tells you things like, "That's where Shakespeare probably walked, or at least thought about walking. That place over there is where he stepped into a dog poo. Probably." It's all very serene and poetic, which is just what you want when you're trying to feel cultured.

And then there's the high street, which is a mix of ancient timber-framed buildings that look like they might fall over if you lean on them too hard, and modern shops where you can buy Shakespeare-themed everything. You've got Shakespeare mugs, Shakespeare t-shirts, probably even Shakespeare socks, which might be what he really would have wanted—a town where you can't even buy a sandwich without being reminded of a soliloquy.

Stratford-upon-Avon is a place where history is practically tripping over itself to get your attention. It's all very charming and twee, like living inside a sonnet, but with more parking problems. It's the kind of town that makes you think, "Yes, I'd like to read more Shakespeare," until you remember that you've already watched *Romeo and Juliet* and decided the ending was a bit of a downer. So, that's Stratford-upon-Avon: where the past is never past, and the present is basically just trying to keep up with the legacy of a bloke who probably never imagined his hometown would end up being a tourist destination with his face on all the tea towels.

13 BIBURY

Bibury. A place that sounds like it might be full of books or maybe some sort of library, but no, it's actually a little village in the Cotswolds that looks like it fell straight out of a fairy tale. If you've ever seen a picture of the Cotswolds, there's a good chance it was of Bibury, because it's got this one row of cottages called Arlington Row that's basically the supermodel of British scenery. They even featured for a while in UK passports. They're so photogenic, they've probably got their own Instagram account by now.

These cottages were built in the 14th century as a wool store, because back then wool was a really big deal. It was like Bitcoin, but fluffier. Then they turned them into weavers' cottages, which is just a fancy way of saying people lived there and made stuff out of wool, probably while complaining about how long it takes to make a jumper. Today, Arlington Row is one of those places where tourists flock to take photos of old houses, and the locals probably wonder why so many people care about where their grandparents used to keep sheep.

Bibury's also got the River Coln running through it, which sounds like something out of a Tolkien novel, but it's just a very pretty river full of very lucky trout. There's even a trout farm, which is like a petting zoo for fish, except you're not really supposed to pet them. You can go there, feed the trout, and then buy some for your dinner, which is a bit awkward if you've just spent time bonding with them.

The whole village looks like it's been frozen in time, which is lovely if you like the past, but probably a bit annoying if you want a decent phone signal. It's got thatched roofs, old stone bridges, and a lot of those little details that make you think, "Wow, I bet they had a really quaint and inconvenient way of doing things back then." The whole place is so pretty that even the tourists get a bit hushed when they visit, like they're worried they might disturb the 17th century.

And then there's St. Mary's Church, which has been there since medieval times, because back then they thought, "If we're going to build something, let's make sure it lasts for at least a thousand years." It's got a proper old graveyard with ancient tombstones that lean at odd angles, like they're just a bit tired of standing around for so long. Inside, there's all sorts of historical stuff to look at, like stained glass windows and carvings of people who've been dead for so long that no one remembers if they were important or just good at donating money to the church.

Bibury is the kind of place that makes you feel like you've stepped into a painting, or maybe a jigsaw puzzle that your nan keeps in the cupboard for special occasions. It's peaceful, picturesque, and slightly surreal, like the sort of village where you'd expect to see a hedgehog wearing a waistcoat. And if you ask anyone from the area, they'll tell you that Bibury was once called "the most beautiful village in England" by William Morris, which is basically like winning a beauty pageant but with more thatched roofs.

So, Bibury: it's ancient, it's adorable, and it's got more ducks and tourists than residents. It's the kind of place that makes you think, "Yes, this is what England is supposed to look like," and then you wonder if you could afford to live there—probably not, but it's nice to dream, isn't it?

14 CASTLE COOMBE

Castle Combe. With a name like that, you'd think it would have a massive castle right in the middle of it, wouldn't you? Like a place where knights would be jousting, and damsels might be needing some rescuing. But no, there's no castle. Not even a tiny one. It's just a really, really pretty village in Wiltshire, where everything looks like it's been designed for a chocolate box or a calendar your gran would hang up in the kitchen.

The "castle" bit comes from a long time ago when there actually was a castle here, but it's been gone for centuries. So now, Castle Combe is all about those classic Cotswold stone houses, narrow streets, and a general feeling that time gave up trying to change anything here around 1600. It's like the village thought, "No, thanks, we're good as we are," and just decided to stay in the past.

And it's proper famous too—Hollywood loves it. They've filmed loads of things here, like *War Horse* and *Stardust*, and probably a few movies about people looking wistfully at fields. Because Castle Combe is the sort of place that makes you feel like you should be wearing a long cloak and staring into the middle distance, thinking about lost love or something.

There's a little market square in the middle, which is really just a bit of cobblestones with a 14th-century market cross stuck in it, reminding you that people have been standing around trying to sell vegetables here for hundreds of years. It's a bit like a medieval shopping mall, except with more thatched roofs and fewer food courts. And there's a cute little church, St. Andrew's, which has a clock inside that's apparently one of the oldest working clocks in the country. It's been ticking away since the 1400s, probably saying, "I can't believe I'm still here" with every chime.

Then there's the river—the Bybrook River. It's not very big or dramatic; it just kind of flows through the village like it's in no rush, which is fitting because nothing in Castle Combe seems to be in much of a rush either. There's a little stone bridge over it that's so photogenic, it could probably do headshots for a living. And people come from all over the world to take pictures of that bridge, as if they've never seen a bridge before.

Castle Combe has been called "the prettiest village in England," which is a bit of a bold claim because there's a lot of pretty villages around, and they all seem to be trying to win some sort of unofficial beauty contest. But it's definitely up there. It's got that vibe where you think, "Yes, this is where they'd film a BBC drama about a vicar who solves crimes." The whole place feels like it's stuck in a very polite time warp, where the biggest excitement is probably if a sheep wanders into the high street.

So, Castle Combe: it's a village that looks like it's been plucked straight out of history and placed gently into the 21st century, but without any of the Wi-Fi or takeaway pizza. It's a place where you go to feel like you're in a simpler time—one where you're more likely to encounter a friendly local or a duck than anything resembling modern life. It's beautiful, it's tiny, and it's definitely not in a hurry to catch up with the rest of the world. And that's what makes it so wonderfully, well, Castle Combe.

15 WARWICK CASTLE

Again, not strictly in the Cotswolds but it's not far from it.
Warwick Castle. It's a proper castle. None of this "well, there
used to be a castle here" business—no, Warwick Castle is the real
deal. It's got towers, turrets, and a massive stone wall, the kind of
place where you'd expect a dragon to turn up, or at least a bloke
in chainmail shouting, "To arms!" It's in Warwick, obviously,
which is in the Midlands, the bit of England that's not quite
north and not quite south, like it couldn't make up its mind.

The castle's been around for over a thousand years, which is ages, even by British history standards. It all kicked off back in 1068 when William the Conqueror decided he needed a big, impressive fortress in the middle of England. You know, just in case anyone got ideas about disagreeing with him. It started as a wooden motte-and-bailey job, which is basically a posh way of saying "giant wooden fence on a hill." But then they upgraded it to stone, because if you're going to build a castle, you might as well make it so solid that it can withstand a few centuries of battles and possibly a medieval tantrum or two.

Warwick Castle's been through all sorts of ups and downs over the years, like some kind of medieval soap opera. There were sieges, battles, and lots of people called "the Earl of Warwick" having arguments about who should sit on the throne. It even played a part in the Wars of the Roses, which was like a medieval family feud but with more armour and less singing.

Today, though, the only battles going on are between tourists for the best spot to take a photo. It's been turned into this massive tourist attraction, a bit like a theme park, but with more history and fewer fast passes. You can see jousting matches, archery displays, and even a giant catapult, which they call a "trebuchet" because that sounds a lot more sophisticated than "big medieval flingy thing"

And if you've ever wanted to know what it's like to be a noble trapped in a castle with nowhere to charge your phone, you can stay in the castle's knight's village. It's all very glamping, with little wooden lodges and pretend medieval touches, but don't worry, they've kept all the modern conveniences, like hot showers and Wi-Fi, because even knights would probably get a bit grumpy without those.

Inside the castle, there's all sorts of grand rooms with chandeliers and armour, and they've got wax figures dressed up like medieval lords and ladies, because apparently, history is more interesting when it's a bit shiny and slightly creepy. You can visit the dungeons too, where they used to lock up people who weren't behaving themselves. Now it's all part of the experience, with actors jumping out to scare you, which is a bit different from the original version, where the scariest thing was being left there for ages.

The Great Hall is where they keep all the swords and suits of armour, because no self-respecting castle would be complete without those. It's like a medieval wardrobe malfunction—lots of metal and definitely not very comfortable. And if you're feeling brave, you can climb the towers, which is basically a way of getting a great view and testing how much you regret that extra scone from the castle café.

Warwick Castle is one of those places where history feels very alive, mainly because there's people running around in costumes yelling about the past. But it's also just a proper impressive castle—big, old, and a bit dramatic. The kind of place that makes you think, "Yes, I could definitely defend this with a longbow," until you realize you'd probably just rather take a nice photo and head to the gift shop for a novelty shield and a plastic sword.

So, Warwick Castle: it's got all the history, all the drama, and all the overpriced snacks you could want from a medieval stronghold. It's a place where you can pretend, just for a bit, that you're living in the 13th century, without having to give up indoor plumbing. And really, that's the best of both worlds, isn't it?

Warwick Castle: Castle Lane, Warwick, Warwickshire, CV34 4QU. www.warwick-castle.com

16 CIRENCESTER

Cirencester. That's a name that sounds like it should be fancy, doesn't it? Like it's the sort of place where you'd find people sipping tea with their pinkies out and talking about the Roman Empire. And actually, that's not too far off, because Cirencester's been around since Roman times, when it was called *Corinium Dobunnorum*, which sounds like a spell from *Harry Potter*. It was a big deal back then—like, the second-largest town in Roman Britain. So, if you think London is old, well, Cirencester was doing its thing long before anyone had even thought about inventing double-decker buses.

Back in Roman days, it had all the mod cons—like a forum, an amphitheatre, and proper roads, which was pretty fancy when most people were still just figuring out fire. The Romans were very into their architecture, so they built these big, straight roads and grand houses with mosaics on the floor, which is like ancient underfloor heating but a lot more artistic. They also had an amphitheatre where they'd gather to watch people shouting and fighting, which is a bit like reality TV but with more actual reality.

These days, you won't see any gladiators in Cirencester, but you can visit the Corinium Museum, which has loads of Roman stuff, like bits of pottery, coins, and those mosaics that look like they'd be really hard to put together if they were a jigsaw puzzle. It's one of those museums where you can see how people used to live back when wearing a toga wasn't just something you did at a stag party.

The town itself is really lovely, in that classic Cotswold way, with all the honey-coloured stone buildings that look like they're permanently stuck in autumn. The Market Place is the heart of Cirencester, and it's been hosting markets since medieval times, which is a really long time to keep selling cabbages. And every week, you can still buy local produce there, except now it's a bit more about organic kale and fancy cheeses than just sheep and turnips.

There's also a massive church, the Parish Church of St. John the Baptist, which is so big they call it a "Cathedral of the Cotswolds," even though it's not technically a cathedral. It's like the church is trying to be extra fancy without having all the qualifications. It's got these beautiful stained-glass windows, ancient tombs, and all those old bits of stone that make you feel like you should whisper, even if you're just trying to find the loo.

Cirencester is surrounded by loads of greenery, because it's right next to the Cotswold Water Park, which isn't like a water park with slides and wave machines—it's actually just loads of lakes where you can go sailing or fishing or pretend you're really into nature for a weekend. It's the sort of place where people bring binoculars and get excited about seeing a rare bird, like a particularly enthusiastic version of *Where's Wally?* but with feathers.

And of course, it's got all the little shops and cafes that you'd expect from a Cotswold town—places where you can buy artisanal bread, expensive candles, and probably a cushion that says something motivational like "Live, Laugh, Fart" in a cursive font. You know, the kind of shops that make you feel like you should be redecorating your living room, even though you just came in for a coffee.

Cirencester's history runs deep, but these days it's more about long walks, cups of tea, and thinking about how nice it must have been to be a Roman, just sitting around in a toga and a pair of sandals. It's a town where the past and the present sort of bump into each other, but very politely, like a couple of tourists at a museum gift shop. Cirencester: ancient, picturesque, and the kind of place that makes you think, "Maybe I should learn more about mosaics."

17 GLOUCESTER

Gloucester. This is a place with a name that sounds like it's got a lot of history, and it really does. It's in Gloucestershire, obviously, which is helpful because otherwise you might forget where it is. Gloucester is one of those cities that's been around since the Romans turned up and decided to build things all over Britain, like baths, roads, and slightly impractical sandals. The Romans called it *Glevum,* which sounds like a type of glue, but actually it was a big Roman town with proper roads, forums, and all those things Romans loved, like straight lines and people wearing togas.

The big thing in Gloucester is the cathedral, Gloucester Cathedral, which is like a giant stone palace for worshipping in. It's been there since around 1089, which is nearly a thousand years ago, give or take a few lost centuries. The cathedral's got all these massive stained-glass windows, intricate carvings, and a ceiling that's so impressive, it makes you want to lie down on the floor just to look at it properly—though they'd probably frown on that. It's famous for its fancy fan-vaulted ceiling, which basically means they made the ceiling look really posh and lacy with stone, because back then, if you didn't make everything look overly complicated, people thought you weren't trying.

The cathedral's also known for being in some of the *Harry Potter* films, which means people come from all over the world to take photos of the cloisters and pretend they're about to cast a spell. It's a bit surreal, really—one minute you're in a medieval church, the next you're hearing a tour guide talking about how many wands Daniel Radcliffe went through on set.

Now, Gloucester's got a proper medieval history too, with all the battles, kings, and mysterious deaths you'd expect. Like King Edward II, who ended up buried in Gloucester Cathedral after being deposed and possibly murdered in a way that you wouldn't talk about at the dinner table. His tomb is still there, and it's got a proper royal feel to it, because even when you're a deposed king, you've still got to look fancy.

The city's right on the River Severn, which is the longest river in Britain, though that's not much of a boast when you realize it's still just a river. It's always been important for trade, because back in the day, rivers were like motorways but slower and wetter. Nowadays, the Gloucester Docks are a big tourist attraction, all revamped with museums, shops, and restaurants, because we love turning places where people used to work really hard into places where we can buy organic coffee.

Gloucester Docks used to be full of ships unloading barrels of cider and other things that people probably got very excited about in the 1800s. Now, it's got the National Waterways Museum, where you can learn all about canals, which is more interesting than it sounds, I promise. And there are lots of converted warehouses, which means you can wander around and feel like you're part of history while trying to find the best place to buy an overpriced sandwich.

It's also got a bit of a rugby obsession—Gloucester Rugby is a huge deal here, with people turning up in cherry-and-white jerseys to shout at each other in the stands at Kingsholm Stadium. Rugby fans in Gloucester take their sport very seriously, like they think it's a matter of life or death, which is exactly the sort of passion you want when the most exciting thing you've got after that is a stroll along the river.

Gloucester's a mix of the really old and the slightly newer, with half-timbered buildings, Roman ruins, and the occasional modern shop that looks a bit out of place. It's the sort of city where you can learn about medieval history, buy a wand, and then sit by the river and think about how much things have changed—or haven't. It's a city that's seen it all, from Roman conquests to students dressed like wizards, and it's still standing strong, like that one pub regular who's seen every fight but never spilled a drop of his pint. So, Gloucester: ancient, a bit quirky, and still trying to figure out what exactly it wants to be, which makes it quite relatable, really.

18 CHELTENHAM

Cheltenham. A place that sounds like it should come with a free glass of champagne and someone offering you a cucumber sandwich. And to be fair, it kind of does. Cheltenham's known as a spa town, which means people used to come here in the 18th century to drink water that tasted weird because they thought it would make them live longer. This was back when people thought bathing was a bit suspicious, so if you found a spring with water that smelled like eggs, you put on your best frock and declared it "medicinal."

It all started when some bloke in 1716 noticed that the local pigeons seemed to love drinking from a mineral spring. And back then, if it was good enough for pigeons, it was good enough for people. So, they built a spa, and suddenly everyone was coming to Cheltenham to drink water that probably tasted a bit like rotten eggs but was considered very posh. It was the 18th-century version of a wellness retreat, except instead of yoga classes, you just sipped sulfuric water and hoped for the best.

Then, in the 19th century, Cheltenham really got its groove on. It became the place where all the rich and fashionable people liked to hang out. They built these grand Regency-style terraces, with white columns and bow windows, like someone decided that houses should look as fancy as possible, even if you just needed a place to store your umbrellas. Now, they're all heritage-listed and people pay loads of money to live in them, even if the ceilings are high enough to lose a balloon in.

Cheltenham is famous for its festivals—it's got more festivals than you can shake a stick at. There's the Cheltenham Literature Festival, where you can go and listen to authors talking about books you haven't read yet, and the Cheltenham Jazz Festival, where you can pretend you understand what a syncopated rhythm is. And then there's the Cheltenham Science Festival, where people try to make complicated things sound fun, like how black holes work or why your phone battery is always on 1% when you need it most.

But the biggest deal in Cheltenham is the horse racing, especially the Cheltenham Festival. It's like the Glastonbury of horse racing, but with more tweed and a lot more betting. And at the centre of it all is the Cheltenham Gold Cup, which is the race that everybody wants to win, unless you're the horse, because you'd probably rather be back in the stable with a carrot. During the Festival, the whole town fills up with people in fancy hats shouting at horses while trying not to spill their champagne. It's the sort of event where you can wear a three-piece suit or a floral dress in March and no one will think you're strange, even if you do have to wade through mud in those posh shoes.

And if you're not into racing or reading, you can always wander around the Montpellier District, which sounds French but is actually just Cheltenham being fancy again. It's full of little boutiques, cafes, and statues of classical figures that make you feel like you should probably know something about Greek mythology. There's even a statue of a hare with antlers called a "jackalope," which is like something out of a storybook but is really just Cheltenham being a bit quirky.

Cheltenham's also known for being the home of GCHQ, which is the government's big, secret listening centre, so if you've ever wondered where all those spies hang out, it's here, right behind a big doughnut-shaped building. They say it's all about national security, but I reckon they might just be trying to listen in on what the horses are saying about the race odds.

So, Cheltenham: it's posh, it's got more festivals than it knows what to do with, and it's all about that sweet spot between history and people pretending they understand jazz. It's a town that's always been trying to be a bit fancier than the rest, whether it's with its spa waters or its elegant terraces, but really, it's just as happy having a bet on a horse and a pint at the pub. And that's what makes it so interesting—like a place where you're never quite sure if you should wear a top hat or just bring an umbrella.

19 GREAT WESTERN STEAM RAILWAY

The Great Western Steam Railway. Simply one of those things that sounds like it should come with a brass band and a man with a twirly moustache shouting "All aboard!" It's proper old-school, back from when trains weren't just a way to get somewhere, but an event. You didn't just catch a train, you *boarded* it, like it was a steam-powered cruise ship on rails.

The Great Western Railway, or GWR if you're in a hurry, was the brainchild of Isambard Kingdom Brunel, who sounds like he should be a character from a historical novel but was actually a real person who liked building massive things. Back in the 19th century, Brunel decided that the British people needed a railway that connected London to the southwest of England and Wales, and he wanted it to be the best railway ever. Because, you know, go big or go home. He even built the tracks to a different gauge than everyone else, making them really wide, which was probably just him showing off a bit, like saying, "My railway's got more space than yours."

The GWR started chugging along in 1838, and soon enough, everyone was talking about how great it was. They even called it the "Great Way Round," which is a bit of a joke because sometimes it did take a longer route, but people didn't mind because they got to ride in fancy carriages with plush seats. It was like the first-class upgrade of its time, except instead of inflight movies, you got to watch the English countryside roll past at a mind-blowing 60 miles an hour. That might not sound fast now, but back then, people probably thought their hats were going to fly off and they'd end up in the next county.

The railway ran all the way from London Paddington down to places like Bristol, Plymouth, and beyond, connecting all those places that were a bit too far away to visit before trains. Suddenly, you could get to the seaside in a few hours instead of spending three days in a horse-drawn carriage feeling like your legs had gone permanently numb. And it wasn't just people that got to travel—loads of goods, like fresh Cornish pasties and Devon cream, could finally reach London without going stale on the way.

Now, Brunel built all sorts of impressive things for the GWR, like tunnels, bridges, and viaducts, because he liked making sure that nature didn't get in the way of his trains. One of the most famous bits is the Box Tunnel, which goes through a hill near Bath and was the longest railway tunnel in the world when it opened. It was so long that people worried they might go in one end and come out the other as a Victorian ghost. But Brunel, being the show-off he was, designed it so that on his birthday, the rising sun shines straight through the tunnel. Because, apparently, he thought, "If I'm going to build a tunnel, I might as well make it magical."

These days, the GWR isn't what it used to be. Most of the steam engines are gone, replaced by electric trains that look like they'd rather be doing your taxes than having a bit of fun. But the Great Western Steam Railway lives on in places like the preserved heritage lines, where you can still ride on a proper steam train, puffing along through the countryside like it's 1890 and you've got all the time in the world. They've got those big steam engines with names like "King Edward II" or "City of Truro," which makes them sound more like royal family members than machines that need a lot of coal to get up a hill.

When you ride one of these steam trains, it's all about the nostalgia—the smell of the coal smoke, the hiss of the steam, and the feeling that you're part of a simpler time when the only thing you had to worry about was whether you'd packed enough sandwiches for the journey. People love it because it makes you feel like a character in an Agatha Christie novel, except hopefully without the murder mystery.

So, the Great Western Steam Railway: it's a bit of history, a bit of engineering genius, and a lot of chuffing noises. It's all about that golden age when travel wasn't just about getting from A to B, but about enjoying the journey, even if you did end up with a bit of soot on your face. And even now, there's just something about a steam train that makes you think, "Yes, this is how travel should be—slow, noisy, and with a proper sense of drama.

Great Western Steam Railway: Winchcombe Railway Station, Winchcombe, Cheltenham, GL54 5LD. www.gwrt.org.uk.

20 COTSWOLD FARM PARK

Cotswold Farm Park. A place where you can go and see animals, but in a way that makes you feel like you're learning something rather than just staring at them. It's in the Cotswolds, obviously, which is that bit of England where everything looks like a postcard and people pretend they've never heard of supermarkets. The Farm Park was started by this bloke called Adam Henson, who's one of those farming types you see on TV, looking very comfortable around sheep and talking about soil like it's the most interesting thing in the world.

Adam's dad, Joe Henson, set up the Cotswold Farm Park back in 1971, which was a time when people had just started to realize that maybe they should stop eating so many endangered animals and start looking after them instead. So, Joe thought, "I'll make a farm where you can see all the rare breeds of farm animals that you never knew you cared about." And it turns out, people really like looking and pointing at animals with funny names, like Gloucester Old Spot pigs or Cotswold Lions, which is actually a type of sheep, not some weird lion-sheep hybrid.

The whole point of the Farm Park is that it's like a zoo, but for animals you're more likely to find in a field than in the Serengeti. It's got sheep, cows, pigs, chickens—basically everything you need to feel like you've stepped back into some romanticized version of farming life, where everything smells like hay instead of manure. But it's not just about looking at the animals. You can get up close and feed them, which makes you feel like a proper farmer, even though you're just holding out a handful of pellets to a very hungry goat that looks like it's considering whether to eat your shoelaces as well.

There's also a lot of baby animals, because who doesn't love a baby animal? They've got lambs, piglets, and calves, which are all just smaller, cuter versions of their grown-up selves. People flock here to watch things like lambing, which is when the sheep give birth, and you get to see a new life enter the world in a slightly sticky way that makes you think, "Oh, that's how that works then." It's educational, but also a bit like a soap opera if you find yourself emotionally invested in whether or not that little lamb is going to take its first steps.

And because it's the Cotswolds, it's all done very nicely. There's a café where you can get a cream tea after you've spent the morning looking at chickens, because nothing says "day out in the countryside" like eating a scone while a sheep bleats in the background. And there's a shop where you can buy local produce, which is like the adult version of bringing back a stick of rock from the seaside—except it's cheese and chutney instead of candy.

They've also got a playground and all those adventure areas for kids, so they can run around and pretend they're little farmers, which is adorable because actual farming involves a lot more getting up early and mucking out barns. There're also tractor rides, which is where you sit on a trailer and get towed around a field while you think, "This must be what it's like to be a turnip."

Cotswold Farm Park is one of those places where you go for a day out, and by the end of it, you're feeling a bit closer to nature, even if the closest you've actually come is petting a very docile rabbit. It's about as wholesome as a loaf of homemade bread, and even if you have no idea what makes a Longhorn cow different from a regular one, you leave thinking, "Maybe I should take up small-scale farming in my back garden."

So, Cotswold Farm Park: it's like a petting zoo, but with a strong educational twist, and a bit of Cotswold flair. It's a place where you can pretend, just for a day, that you understand the countryside life—without actually having to shovel anything. And you get to learn just enough about rare breeds to impress your friends at the pub, which, in the end, is what most of us are really looking for.

Cotswold Farm Park: Guiting Power, Cheltenham, Gloucestershire, GL54 5FL. www.cotswoldfarmpark.co.uk. T: +44 (0)1451 850307.

21 THE SLAUGHTERS

Upper and Lower Slaughter. Now, those are some village names that sound like they should come with a horror movie rating, but actually, they're just a couple of the prettiest, most peaceful places in the Cotswolds. You hear the name "Slaughter" and you think, "Blimey, that must have been where all sorts of gruesome things happened," but no—turns out it comes from an old English word *slohtre*, which means "muddy place." So, it's less "Axe Murderer Town" and more "Muddy Footpath Village."

The Slaughters are a bit like a pair of twins—Upper Slaughter and Lower Slaughter. They're right next to each other, only separated by about a mile, which is perfect if you fancy a very short walk but still want to tell people you've visited two different villages. The River Eye runs through both of them, which is basically a small stream pretending to be a river, but it looks very picturesque with little stone bridges arching over it, like something out of a chocolate box that your aunt would buy at the garden centre.

Let's start with Lower Slaughter, which has a watermill that's become one of the most photographed spots in the Cotswolds. It's all very idyllic, with a little wheel turning and a café inside that makes scones. You can stand by the river and think, "Ah, this is what England is all about," even if it does mean you're standing in the middle of a load of tourists taking photos of the same thing. It's the kind of village where you expect to see a duck wandering around wearing a bow tie, or a local vicar writing poetry under a willow tree.

Upper Slaughter is just up the hill a bit, and it's got a bit of a posher vibe. It calls itself a "Doubly Thankful Village," which sounds like it's showing off, but it actually means something quite nice. It's one of those places that didn't lose anyone in either World War, which is pretty rare and makes you feel like the whole village is charmed or blessed or something. It's all very serene, with cottages that look like they've been built out of gingerbread and a church that's just the right amount of wonky from being around for hundreds of years.

What's funny about the Slaughters is that even though they're right next to each other, they're both really tiny, like they just couldn't bear to be apart but didn't want to merge into one slightly bigger village. There's no big shops or supermarkets, just a handful of old houses, a couple of B&Bs, and the sort of quiet that makes you wonder if you've accidentally wandered into a museum exhibit about village life. And yet, people come from all over the world just to walk between them, because they're like the ultimate in Cotswold charm—quaint, peaceful, and with names that sound much more dramatic than they actually are.

So, that's Upper and Lower Slaughter: not nearly as murderous as they sound, but very good at looking like something from a storybook. They're places where nothing much happens, which is exactly why people love them. You can take a stroll along the river, have a cream tea, and feel like you've travelled back in time, all while being in a place called "Slaughter" that's never seen anything scarier than a rogue hedgehog. It's a bit confusing, but that's the English countryside for you—always doing the opposite of what you'd expect.

22 BURFORD GARDEN CENTRE

Burford Garden Centre. So, you might think a garden centre is just a place where you buy a few begonias, maybe a nice terracotta pot, and then go home to try and keep everything alive. But Burford Garden Centre is on a whole different level. It's not just a garden centre—it's like the Buckingham Palace of garden centres, with a bit of posh retail therapy thrown in. It's where people go when they want to feel like they're improving their garden *and* their lifestyle, all while enjoying a nice slice of cake.

When you walk into Burford Garden Centre, you quickly realize it's not just about the plants. Oh, no. You can buy plants, of course—loads of them, in fact. There's everything from tiny succulents to trees that look like they'd need their own postcode. But that's just the beginning. It's got furniture, homewares, clothes, and even a food hall, because clearly, there's nothing that gets you in the mood for a new set of patio chairs like a selection of artisanal cheeses.

And this place is big. It's like the TARDIS of garden centres— looks like a regular greenhouse from the outside, but inside it just keeps going. You wander through one section of houseplants, thinking you've seen everything, and then suddenly you're in an entire area dedicated to outdoor fire pits, like they think every garden in Britain could double as a campsite. And they've got rows and rows of books about gardening, cooking, mindfulness—basically anything that makes you feel like you're improving yourself, even if you just end up buying a novelty birdhouse.

And then there's the café. Well, calling it a café feels a bit rude, really—it's more of a restaurant that happens to be inside a garden centre. You can get fancy brunches, cakes that look like they've been designed for a baking show, and coffee served in those rustic mugs that make you feel like you're sitting in a cozy cottage, even though you're actually in a giant glass building. It's the kind of place where you can overhear people talking about the best way to compost, while they're eating an almond croissant that probably cost more than your first car.

The food hall is like a farmer's market but with air conditioning and a much higher price tag. It's filled with local produce, fancy jams, posh chocolates, and cheeses that come with a backstory. They even have their own bakery, which means you can buy a loaf of sourdough and convince yourself that you're living the artisan life, even if you still can't remember to water your plants. It's like a mini-Harrods, but instead of walking out with a designer handbag, you leave with a selection of organic chutneys and a new pair of secateurs.

Burford Garden Centre is one of those places that makes you feel like you should be better at gardening than you actually are. You see all these beautifully arranged plants and start to imagine your own garden looking like a feature in a lifestyle magazine. But deep down, you know that in a few weeks, you'll be looking at a couple of wilted leaves and wondering where it all went wrong. Still, it's worth a visit, even if you end up spending more time in the home décor section than actually looking at the plants.

So, Burford Garden Centre: it's not just a place to buy a pot for your geranium. It's more like a day out where you can buy a scented candle that smells like optimism and a new pair of gardening gloves that will definitely make you more productive (even if they won't). It's posh, it's polished, and it's basically a theme park for people who think they might want to plant a hydrangea, but mostly just want to sit down with a nice cup of tea. And honestly, that's the best kind of garden centre, isn't it?

Burford Garden Centre: Shilton Road, Burford, Oxon, OX18 4PA. www.burford.co.uk. T: +44 (0)1993 823117.

23 GLOUCESTER MOTORWAY SERVICES

Gloucester Motorway Services. You hear the words "motorway services," and you probably think of a depressing stretch of tarmac, a coffee machine that's never quite working, and a tired-looking Greggs. But Gloucester Services is nothing like that. No, it's the *Waitrose* of motorway services, the fancy pants rest stop where even the petrol pumps feel like they've been tastefully curated. It's right on the M5, between Gloucester and Cheltenham, and it's like they thought, "Why should people suffer just because they're on a long drive?"

Most motorway services are designed to make you want to leave as quickly as possible, but Gloucester Services is the kind of place where you might accidentally spend an hour just looking at jars of chutney. It's got big, glass walls that let you see the rolling hills outside, which is handy if you need to remind yourself that there's a world beyond the inside of your car. They've even put a grassy roof on it, so from above it looks like it's just blending into the landscape, as if it's embarrassed about being a services and is trying to hide.

Inside, it's like a little slice of the Cotswolds, but with toilets. They've got a farm shop that's more like a posh deli, filled with local produce, artisan cheeses, handmade pies, and all sorts of things you probably didn't realize you needed while driving down the M5. You can buy freshly baked bread and proper butchers' meat, because nothing says "road trip" like thinking about what you're going to cook when you get home. It's the sort of place where you can stock up on fancy sausages while pretending you're just taking a quick loo break.

And the food! This is no sad burger in a limp bun. You've got a deli counter, fresh salads, hot meals that wouldn't look out of place in a gastropub, and cakes that are probably better than anything you'd find in most villages. It's got all those rustic touches, like wooden tables and exposed beams, so you can sit there eating your locally sourced sausage roll while feeling like you're in some sort of woodland retreat, even though you're actually just a few feet away from a coachload of people in matching tracksuits.

They've even got a play area for kids that doesn't look like it's made out of indestructible plastic and broken dreams but instead has wooden climbing frames and a bit of green space. It's all very wholesome, like they've decided that just because you're stuck on a long journey with your children doesn't mean you have to suffer more than necessary.

It's not cheap, of course—nothing that involves the words "artisanal," "locally-sourced," or "Cotswold honey" ever is. But people don't mind paying a bit extra here, because it makes them feel like they're better than just pulling over for a service station burger. They get to feel like they're part of the slow food movement, even if they've still got 200 miles to go and just want to buy a nice pork pie to munch in the car.

Gloucester Services has won loads of awards, which is probably a bit strange if you think about it, because it's still just a place to get fuel and use the loo. But it's a bit of a celebrity in the world of motorway stops—like the Adele of rest areas. It's what happens when people take something that's usually quite grim and decide to make it really, really nice, like if someone turned a port-a-loo into a five-star bathroom.

So, Gloucester Motorway Services: it's more than just a pit stop, it's an experience. It's where you can buy a freshly baked pasty, some hand-crafted soap, and a bag of organic apples, all while forgetting you're right next to the M5. It's not just a place to stretch your legs, it's a place to stretch your expectations of what a service station can be. And that's quite something, really, isn't it?

Gloucester Motorway Services: M5 motorway (between J12 and 11a), Brookthorpe, Gloucestershire, GL4 0DN. Gloucesterservices.com.

24 CHASTLETON HOUSE

Chastleton House. A place that sounds like it should have a ghost or two rattling about, doesn't it? It's one of those grand old country houses tucked away in the Cotswolds, where everything looks like it's been left exactly as it was when Queen Victoria was still getting used to the idea of tea. It's a proper Jacobean mansion, built in the early 1600s, and it's been standing there, minding its own business, for over 400 years, which is longer than most of us manage to keep a houseplant alive.

The house was built by a bloke named Walter Jones, who clearly thought, "I've got all this money, why not build a massive house and fill it with stuff?" And that's exactly what he did. Chastleton House is like a time capsule, but instead of burying it in the ground, they just put a roof over it and left it to gather dust. It stayed in the same family for almost 400 years, which means they didn't have much time for redecorating, so you've got bits of furniture and wallpaper that have seen better days but in a way that makes them look charming rather than just knackered.

Walking through Chastleton House is a bit like wandering through your great-aunt's attic—everything's old, a bit faded, and it all looks like it's got a story, but nobody's quite sure what that story is anymore. It's got those creaky floorboards that sound like they're complaining with every step, and rooms that are all slightly wonky because, back in the day, builders didn't bother too much about things like "straight lines."

There's a Great Hall, which is basically a big room where they used to show off to visitors. It's got a massive fireplace that looks like you could roast an entire sheep in it, which is probably what they did back in the day when they got the munchies. And the Long Gallery upstairs is the longest one in England, which is quite a niche record to hold, but there you go. It's where people used to walk back and forth, thinking about how great they were and probably playing games that involved wearing very uncomfortable shoes.

Speaking of games, Chastleton House is famous for being where they wrote the rules of modern croquet, which is a game that sounds a lot more exciting than it actually is. Imagine Victorian gentlemen standing around in their stiff collars, arguing about how many hoops a proper game should have. It's a bit like the Wimbledon of the 19th century, but with less running and more arguing over whose ball went through the hoop first.

The garden outside is as old as the house, and it's got that slightly overgrown look that makes it seem like nature's trying to take back control but hasn't quite managed it yet. There's a topiary garden, which is basically a fancy way of saying "bushes cut into weird shapes," and a kitchen garden that's been around since people thought growing your own vegetables was just what you did, rather than a trendy lifestyle choice.

The National Trust runs the place now, which means you can go and have a wander around while wearing one of those stickers that prove you've paid to see history. And because it's the National Trust, they've kept it all exactly as it is, cobwebs and all, so you get a real sense of what life was like when people thought electric lighting was the stuff of science fiction. They haven't spruced it up or made it fancy—it's just there, slightly worn around the edges, like your favourite old jumper that has more holes than wool but you still love it.

Chastleton House is one of those places where you can imagine all sorts of dramas playing out—affairs, arguments, secret letters, and maybe the odd duel in the garden. But mostly, it's just a big, quiet house, sitting in the countryside, as if it's not entirely sure what happened to the last few centuries. It's grand but not too grand, a bit dusty but in a way that makes you think, "Yes, this is how history should be." It's the kind of house that's been around so long, it's stopped caring about impressing anyone, and honestly, that's what makes it brilliant.

Chastleton House: www.nationaltrust.org.uk/visit/oxfordshire-buckinghamshire-berkshire/chastleton

25 BLOCKLEY

Blockley. It's a village name that sounds like it could be a bit tough, doesn't it? Like it's made out of bricks and concrete. But actually, Blockley is about as quaint and charming as it gets, tucked away in the Cotswolds where everything looks like it's been designed to make you say, "Ah, lovely," every five minutes. It's one of those villages where time seems to have stopped about 200 years ago, but everyone's happy about it because, let's face it, the past looks a lot better when you've got central heating.

Back in the day, Blockley was all about the wool trade, because that's what the Cotswolds was built on—sheep with really great hair. The village got rich from weaving and spinning and all that, and you can still see the old mill buildings around the place, though they're not filled with people working hard anymore. Nowadays, they're more likely to be posh flats or little workshops where people make artisanal candles that smell like freshly cut grass.

But Blockley didn't stop with wool. It had a second act in the 18th and 19th centuries when it became a big name in the silk industry. That's right—silk, like the fancy stuff they use for dressing up. They even had their own silkworms, which is basically farming but with much smaller livestock. Picture all these Victorian types standing around, looking very serious about their silk production, while the silkworms just chewed on mulberry leaves and got on with it. And when the silk trade dried up, the village went back to being a sleepy little spot in the hills, which is probably what it wanted all along.

Today, Blockley is one of those Cotswold villages that looks like it's been plucked straight out of a period drama, which it sort of has, because they film *Father Brown* here. That's the TV show about a priest who solves crimes, which is handy if you like the idea of your murder mysteries with a bit more tea and moral guidance. You can wander around the village and spot all the places where they've filmed, like St. Peter and St. Paul's Church, and imagine yourself in a scene where someone says, "It was the vicar with the candlestick, in the old mill."

The church itself is a proper piece of history, dating back to the 12th century, which means it's seen all sorts of changes—plagues, wars, people swapping out pews for comfier chairs. It's got those gravestones that lean at strange angles like they're having a gossip session about how much better the 14th century was.

Blockley is also great if you like a nice walk, because it's surrounded by hills and woodlands, with loads of footpaths that go up and down like they think you need the exercise. The village is in this little valley, and it's got a brook running through it, which is just a posh word for a small river. It's one of those places where you can hear water burbling away in the background, and it makes everything feel even more peaceful, unless you're the sort of person who always needs Wi-Fi to feel calm.

There's a couple of pubs, of course, because it wouldn't be a Cotswold village without somewhere to get a pint after all that walking. They've got those cosy interiors where you can sit by a log fire and pretend you're in the 1800s, except now you've got a locally brewed ale instead of whatever questionable drink people used to make out of fermented turnips.

Blockley isn't a big tourist hotspot like some of its Cotswold neighbours, but that's kind of the point. It's more of a hidden gem, like the Cotswolds' best-kept secret, except everyone who's been there probably tells their friends about it because it's so nice. It's the kind of place where you can just sit on a bench, look at a stone cottage covered in ivy, and think, "Yes, I could live here." Even if you couldn't really afford it, because let's face it, everywhere in the Cotswolds costs more than a small castle these days.

So, Blockley: it's small, it's historic, and it's about as peaceful as a village can get while still having a couple of tea rooms and a corner shop. It's got that perfect mix of old mills, stone cottages, and a general sense that time moves just a little bit slower here. It's the kind of place where even the sheep probably have a better quality of life than most of us, and honestly, that's part of its charm.

26 THE ROLLRIGHT STONES

The Rollright Stones. Sounds like they should be a band from the 60s that didn't quite make it big, but actually, it's a bunch of ancient rocks in the middle of the Oxfordshire countryside. It's one of those mysterious places that's been around for so long, no one really knows why it's there, but that hasn't stopped people from making up all sorts of theories about it over the years. It's like the British answer to Stonehenge, but smaller, with fewer tourists, and a bit less smug about being on postcards.

The Rollright Stones are actually three separate things: the King's Men, the King Stone, and the Whispering Knights. Sounds like they should all be characters in a fantasy novel, but they're just standing stones that have been sitting in a field for about 4,000 years, not doing much except confusing people. They're made of that lovely old limestone that looks like it's been through a few thousand years of British weather—which it has—and they're all a bit wonky and moss-covered, like they've just given up trying to stand straight.

The King's Men is a big stone circle, sort of like Stonehenge's little brother who's never quite had the same attention but is doing its best. It's a circle of about 70 or so stones (no one can quite agree on the exact number), all huddled together like they're having a very long meeting that no one can remember the agenda for. The story goes that if you try to count the stones, you'll never get the same number twice, which sounds more like a problem with counting than with the stones, but it adds to the mystery, doesn't it?

Then there's the King Stone, which is this tall, thin rock that looks a bit like it's trying to be a headstone but got tired halfway through. The legend says it's a king who was turned into stone by a witch, which is exactly the sort of thing people used to say back when they didn't have the internet to look up the actual reasons. Apparently, the king was on his way to conquer England when the witch stopped him and said,

> *Seven long strides thou shalt take, says she*
> *And if Long Compton thou canst see,*
> *King of England thou shalt be!*

He took the steps but couldn't see Long Compton which was inconveniently hiding behind another hill. The witch cackled (probably):

As Long Compton thou canst not see, King of England thou shalt not be! Rise up stick and stand still stone, For King of England thou shalt be none; Thou and thy men hoar stones shall be, And I myself an elder tree!

So turned to stone was he, and you can point at him today and laugh at his misfortune. Just don't try to step forward and see Long Compton for yourself, or you too may be turned to stone (or something).

And then you've got the Whispering Knights, which is a little cluster of stones that look like they're having a secret chat, probably about how the King Stone has gone a bit power mad. They're supposed to be a group of knights plotting against their king, which is a great story if you ignore the fact that they've just been sitting there, being rocks, for thousands of years. They're a bit fallen over and worn down, like they've been whispering for so long they've run out of things to say.

People love to say the Rollright Stones are all magical or have some sort of special energy. You know, that whole "aligns with the solstice" and "feels really mystical" sort of thing. Which is just a nice way of saying, "We have no idea why they're here, but it's a bit weird, isn't it?" Some people think the stones have healing powers, which is great if you believe that sitting near a rock can sort out your back pain. Others reckon the place is full of ancient pagan vibes, like druids used to dance around the stones wearing robes and chanting, but really, they probably just argued about who had the best beard.

Archaeologists think the stones might have been used for ancient rituals or burials, which is pretty much their default guess whenever they find old rocks in a field. But no one's entirely sure, because the people who put the stones there didn't bother to leave any instructions. They just left them standing in a field and wandered off, leaving future generations to wonder, "Why did they bother?"

So, the Rollright Stones: they're ancient, they're mysterious, and they're a bit of a puzzle. It's the sort of place where you can stand around, looking thoughtful, and pretend you know what Neolithic people were up to, even though you're really just hoping your phone's got enough signal to Google it. It's a bit eerie, a bit magical, and a lot older than anything else you'll find around these parts. And that's what makes it brilliant—no one knows exactly what's going on, but we're all very happy to keep guessing.

Rollright Stones: Rollright Road, Little Rollright, Oxfordshire, OX7 5QB. www.rollrightstones.co.uk.

27 SHIPSTON ON STOUR

Shipston-on-Stour. That's a name that's doing a lot of heavy lifting. It's a town, and it's on the River Stour, which is good to know in case you get lost and need to ask a local where you are. They'll say, "You're in Shipston, on the Stour," and you'll think, "Ah yes, that clears things up nicely." It's one of those places that sounds like it should have a proud history, and it does, but mostly about things like washing sheep and occasionally wondering why anyone would build a town in a place where it rains so much.

Back in medieval times, Shipston-on-Stour was all about sheep. In fact, the name comes from "Sheep-wash-town," which tells you exactly what they got up to here. Apparently, people used to bring their sheep down to the river for a good wash before selling them, because no one wants a dirty sheep, do they? You could probably charge extra for a sheep with that fresh, river-clean scent. But the sheep-washing days are long gone, and now the river's just there for a nice view and for people to throw bread at the ducks.

These days, Shipston is a classic market town—you know, the sort of place where there's a market once a week, and people still think it's the biggest event on the calendar. Market day is Friday, and you can buy all sorts of things, from local produce to homemade jam, and maybe even some woolly socks as a nod to the town's sheepy past. The market's been going for centuries, and it's the sort of place where you can hear phrases like "a good crop of parsnips this year" and feel like you've just walked into an episode of *The Archers*.

The town's got a high street, and it's exactly what you'd expect from a Cotswold town—stone buildings, little independent shops, and a few places where you can buy organic coffee because apparently, even in the middle of the countryside, people need their flat whites. There's also a Co-op, because no matter how picturesque a place is, people still need somewhere to buy toilet roll and a loaf of bread.

St. Edmund's Church is right in the middle of town, looking like it's been around forever—which it sort of has. It's one of those old churches with a tower that's probably seen everything from the Black Death to the invention of the selfie stick. Inside, it's all ancient pews and stained glass, and that smell of old stone that every church seems to have, like it's been storing up centuries of rain and hope. It's the kind of place that makes you feel like you should lower your voice, even if you're just saying, "Blimey, it's chilly in here."

Shipston's also known as the gateway to the Cotswolds, which is what towns say when they're on the edge of somewhere more famous. It's the kind of place where tourists pass through on their way to see rolling hills and cute villages, but sometimes they stop off to see what all the fuss is about. And they find a town that's just busy enough to be interesting, but quiet enough that the biggest news might be someone's cat going missing for a few hours.

And because it's near the Cotswolds, there's loads of lovely countryside walks around Shipston. You can wander along footpaths, through fields, past hedgerows, and maybe spot a few sheep who are blissfully unaware that their ancestors were once scrubbed clean in the town's river. It's the sort of walk where you end up back at the local pub with muddy boots and a sense of achievement, even though you've mostly just been following a path and wondering how long it's acceptable to spend in a pub on a Sunday afternoon.

Shipston-on-Stour might not be the biggest place, but it's got a proper community vibe—the kind where people know your business before you've even finished doing it. There're all sorts of local events, like summer fairs, and if you're new, you'll probably find yourself invited to something within a week. It's friendly like that, in the way that small towns are when they want to know if you're planning to stay or just passing through.

So, Shipston-on-Stour: it's a town that's ancient but not ancient enough to have its own museum of Roman artefacts. It's got history, charm, and just enough sheep references to keep things interesting. It's the sort of place where time moves a bit slower, and that's just how they like it. If you want a taste of proper English village life, but with a good cup of coffee and a few polite nods to modernity, then this is the place to be. It's not just on the Stour—it's on the map. Sort of.

28 WOODSTOCK (INC BLENHEIM PALACE)

Woodstock. Most people think of as a massive music festival full of hippies back in the '60s. But this Woodstock isn't about peace, love, and rock 'n' roll—no, this is a small market town in Oxfordshire, near the Cotswolds, where things are a bit more *posh* and a lot less muddy. It's the sort of place where the wildest thing that might happen is a particularly rowdy game of croquet.

Woodstock's got history dripping out of it—like, loads of history, just lying around for anyone to trip over. The town's been around since the medieval days, and its name comes from the old

English words for "clearing in the woods," which is exactly the sort of thing people used to think was interesting before Netflix came along. Back then, this place was a favourite of kings and queens, because royalty loved a good clearing, especially if it came with a nice bit of hunting land nearby.

And speaking of royalty, Woodstock's home to Blenheim Palace, which is one of those big country houses that's so huge, you could get lost in it for days and probably still not find the kitchen. Blenheim Palace is a UNESCO World Heritage site, which means it's one of those places that the rest of the world thinks is important too. It was built in the 18th century as a thank-you present to the Duke of Marlborough for winning some battles, which is a bit different from getting a gold watch at retirement, isn't it? They just handed him an entire palace and some nice gardens.

It's also the birthplace of Winston Churchill, which means there's a whole room in Blenheim Palace dedicated to him and his cigars. They'll tell you all about how he was born in a small room there, which is ironic, because he then spent the rest of his life being larger than life and making speeches that went on a bit. You can visit the palace, wander around the fancy state rooms, and look at portraits of people who probably never had to worry about paying their gas bill.

But Woodstock isn't just about Blenheim—it's got its own little charm, too. The town's full of those classic stone buildings that look like they've been there since the dawn of time, or at least since the last time anyone thought "minimalism" was a good idea. There's a proper market square with a town hall, because back in the day, every respectable town needed a place to shout about turnip prices. Now, it's the kind of square where you might find a nice farmers' market, selling locally-sourced honey and artisanal bread that costs more than your car.

Woodstock's got plenty of little shops and antique stores, which is great if you like browsing through other people's old stuff and convincing yourself that what you really need is a vintage teapot that you'll never actually use. There's also a bunch of cosy pubs, where you can sit with a pint and think about how many famous people have passed through Woodstock over the centuries. They've probably sat in the same spot, but with fewer Wi-Fi options.

And it's a great place for a walk, if you're into that sort of thing. You can stroll around the beautiful grounds of Blenheim, where everything's been landscaped to look like nature's just trying its best, even though there's a team of gardeners making sure every tree knows its place. Or you can head into the town and wander down little lanes that make you feel like you've walked onto the set of a period drama where nothing bad ever happens, except maybe a misunderstanding at the village bake sale.

Woodstock is also one of those places that's very good at pretending it's not part of the modern world. It's got that timeless feel, where the biggest excitement is a new exhibit at the local museum or a particularly nice afternoon tea. But it's not boring—it's more like it's chosen to stick with the best bits of the past, while letting the rest of the world rush about and stress out about Wi-Fi speeds.

So, Woodstock: it's old, it's beautiful, and it's got more history than you can shake a very ancient stick at. It's the kind of place that makes you want to speak in a slightly posher accent, even if you don't know what you're talking about. It's where you can pretend you're a lord or lady, at least until you realise that your day pass to the palace is running out. And honestly, isn't that what we're all looking for in a day out? A bit of fantasy, a lot of scenery, and a nice cup of tea at the end of it.

Blenheim Palace: Blenheim Palace, Woodstock, Oxfordshire, OX20 1UL. www.blenheimpalace.com.

29 OXFORD

Oxford. Isn't it a place that just sounds clever? Like, if you say "Oxford" enough times, you might accidentally learn Latin or figure out how gravity works. It's one of those cities that's so famous for being intelligent, you'd think the air itself might give you an extra A-level just by breathing it in. It's home to the University of Oxford, which is like the grandparent of all universities, being around for nearly a thousand years. If you think your school was strict, imagine a place where they've been studying for that long—they're practically professionals at being professional.

The university's made up of a bunch of different colleges, like a posh student housing situation, but instead of just renting a flat, you get to live in a building that's older than most countries. There're colleges with names like Balliol, Magdalen (which is pronounced "Maudlin" because, you know, Oxford), and Christ Church, which sounds more like a religious experience than a place where people are still pulling all-nighters before exams. Each college has its own dining hall, its own library, and its own set of rules, which just adds to the whole atmosphere of, "Yes, you're very lucky to be here, but don't touch the ancient books without permission."

Christ Church College is the one that really shows off, though. It's got its own cathedral—because, why not?—and a dining hall that looks suspiciously like the one from *Harry Potter*. And that's because it actually *is* the one from *Harry Potter,* sort of. They filmed bits of the movies there, which means tourists flock in with their cameras and scarves, even though most of the students are just trying to eat breakfast without someone pretending they're about to be sorted into Hufflepuff.

The Bodleian Library is another one of those places that's so old and fancy that you're not allowed to take books out of it. Because when you're in a library that's been collecting books since the 1600s, you can't trust people not to lose a first edition of something really important. It's like a museum for books, but one where people actually still sit down to read, because they haven't yet figured out that most of those books are probably online by now. There's a bit called the Radcliffe Camera, which is not a camera at all, but a round building where students study while tourists take photos outside and wonder what it would be like to be that clever.

But Oxford isn't just about the university—though it's kind of hard to avoid it, seeing as the university takes up half the city. It's also got loads of museums, like the Ashmolean, which is a big, impressive building full of old stuff. It's the oldest public museum in Britain, which means it's been around long enough to collect everything from ancient Egyptian mummies to paintings of people you've never heard of but who look very serious. It's the kind of museum where you pretend to appreciate the art, but really you're just trying to find the café.

And then there's the river, the Thames, but in Oxford they like to call it the Isis, because calling it the same name as everyone else would be far too simple. People go punting on the river, which is like a boat ride, but with more chance of falling in because you're using a big pole to push yourself along. It's all very picturesque, and you'll see loads of students in striped blazers pretending it's not as hard as it looks, while tourists take photos of them drifting into the bushes.

The city itself is full of those beautiful stone buildings that make you feel like you should be writing poetry or having deep thoughts about philosophy. You wander down streets with names like "Logic Lane" and "Turl Street," and you can't help but feel a little bit smarter, even if you're just looking for somewhere that sells decent sandwiches. And there's the Covered Market, which is a bit like a shopping centre, but one where all the shops are crammed together and it's been around since the 18th century, so you can buy artisanal bread and fancy tea while imagining you're in a Dickens novel.

Oxford's got a lot going on—there's theatres, bookshops, and little pubs where you can sit down with a pint and wonder if you're sitting in the same spot where some genius came up with a groundbreaking theory, or if you're just on the stool they always reserve for tourists. The Eagle and Child is one of the famous pubs, where J.R.R. Tolkien and C.S. Lewis used to meet and chat about hobbits and lions and whatnot, like they were just ordinary blokes having a chat over a beer, except they were also reinventing literature.

So, Oxford: it's old, it's brainy, and it's got more history than you could shake a thesis at. It's the sort of place that makes you think, "Yes, maybe I'll just pop into the library and casually read some ancient manuscripts." But really, you'll probably just end up on an open-topped bus tour, staring at college gates that you're not allowed through, and wondering if any of that intellectual brilliance might rub off on you if you hang around long enough. And that's the magic of Oxford—it makes everyone feel a little bit smarter, even if you're just there for the scones.

30 SUDELEY CASTLE

Sudeley Castle is in a little town called Winchcombe, which sounds like the kind of place where people still use words like "ye olde" and think a bit of rain is character-building. The castle's been around since the 15th century, but the site goes back even further, because if there's one thing the British love, it's building new castles on top of old things. It's like they were trying to set a high score for "most history in one place."

Sudeley is most famous for being the home of Katherine Parr, the sixth wife of Henry VIII—the one who didn't get her head chopped off, which, let's face it, makes her the real winner of that particular game. She outlived Henry, which was quite a feat given his tendency to solve marital disputes with an axe, and she ended up living here at Sudeley Castle. She even died here, which is less cheerful but very historic, and she's buried in the chapel on the castle grounds, which makes her the only queen buried on private land in England. That's like a very posh, very permanent Airbnb.

Sudeley's also seen its fair share of royal drama. There're stories about Edward IV, Richard III, and even Elizabeth I hanging around, which just goes to show that if you want a castle to stay relevant, you need to get as many royals as possible through the door. It's like they were collecting them like football stickers— got to catch them all! Elizabeth I even had a bit of a holiday here, probably enjoying a bit of peace before heading back to London where everyone kept asking her about marriage.

During the English Civil War, Sudeley Castle had a bit of a rough time, because castles back then were basically like medieval piñatas—if you whacked them hard enough, you got to keep whatever was inside. The Royalists and Parliamentarians took turns bashing it up, and by the end of it, Sudeley was left in ruins, which is what happens when two sides decide that your home makes a great target. It just sat there, being all picturesque and crumbling, until the 19th century when a rich family called the Dent-Brocklehursts (yes, that's a real name) decided to buy it and do a bit of a fixer-upper.

Today, Sudeley Castle is one of those places where you can go for a day out and feel like you're learning something while secretly just wanting to see if there's a café with scones. It's got beautiful gardens, because every proper castle needs a garden where you can pretend to be a medieval noble having a stroll. There's rose gardens, herb gardens, and even a knot garden, which is basically a garden where all the plants look like they've been put through a giant braid. They're the sort of gardens that make you think, "Yes, I should really get into gardening," until you remember that you can't even keep a basil plant alive.

Inside the castle, it's all about grand rooms with tapestries, ancient portraits, and a faint musty smell that makes you feel like you're breathing in a bit of the past. There're suits of armour dotted about, which is exactly what you'd expect from a castle. It's like they're saying, "Yes, knights really did live here," even though the closest thing to a knight you'll see nowadays is a tour guide in a slightly rumpled uniform.

They've also got a collection of artifacts, which is a posh word for "old stuff people have found and decided to keep." You can see things like Katherine Parr's prayer book, which is a bit like an ancient version of a Kindle, except much harder to carry around. There're also exhibitions about the history of the place, complete with information panels that make you feel like you're doing something educational, even if you're mostly just looking for the gift shop.

Speaking of gift shops, the one at Sudeley is exactly what you'd expect—full of books about the Tudors, little jars of fancy jam, and probably a tea towel with the family crest on it, because nothing says "I've been to a historic castle" like a tea towel that costs more than a supermarket multipack.

So, Sudeley Castle: it's old, it's grand, and it's got more royal connections than an episode of *The Crown*. It's the sort of place that makes you feel like you've stepped back in time, even if the past is mostly just a bit drafty and full of people in ruffs. It's got history, gardens, and enough legends to keep the ghost hunters interested. And if you're lucky, you might even find a quiet corner where you can sit down and imagine what it would have been like to be a queen—just without the risk of losing your head.

Sudeley Castle: Sudeley Castle & Gardens, Winchcombe, Gloucestershire, GL54 5JD. www.sudeleycastle.co.uk

31 TETBURY

Tetbury. It's a place that sounds like it should come with its own royal warrant, doesn't it? Like you might turn up and find King Charles whispering to a spider plant, or something. And, actually, you wouldn't be far off, because Tetbury is in the Cotswolds, and it's got more royal connections than the guest list at a Buckingham Palace garden party. It's one of those market towns where everything looks like it's been arranged to be on the cover of a jigsaw puzzle called *Quaint British Villages*.

Tetbury's been around since the Middle Ages, and back then it was all about wool, because if there's one thing the Cotswolds has always had a lot of, it's sheep. The whole town made its money from selling wool, which means it's got one of those old market halls with a pointy roof and arches that make it look like a very fancy sheep shelter. They've been holding markets here for centuries, which just shows that people in Tetbury have always been good at getting other people to buy things.

These days, the market's a bit more about antiques than sheep. Tetbury is like the antiques capital of the Cotswolds—there are more antique shops here than you'd think possible for a place with only a few thousand people. It's the sort of town where you can pop in for a loaf of bread and come out with a Victorian lamp, a Georgian chair, and a vague feeling that you should have been born in a different century. The antiques are probably more valuable than the average house, but that's just part of the charm, isn't it? It's like a museum where everything's for sale.

But Tetbury's real claim to fame is its royal neighbour: King Charles. His Highgrove Estate is just down the road, where he grows all sorts of organic things, like vegetables, flowers, and opinions about architecture. Highgrove's got this fancy garden that people love to visit, because there's nothing quite like paying to look at a royal vegetable patch. You can't just wander in, of course—you have to book in advance, which is exactly the kind of thing you'd expect from a royal garden. It's all very tasteful and natural, like they're trying to show that, yes, even kings care about bees.

Because of its royal connection, Tetbury has become one of those places where you might bump into someone famous buying jam in the local deli, or at least spot a Range Rover that looks like it might belong to someone important. The high street's full of little boutiques selling things like artisanal soaps, cashmere scarves, and chutney that costs more than your average vacation. It's the kind of place where even the charity shops look like they've been curated by interior designers.

And it's got some proper history too, like the Parish Church of St. Mary the Virgin and St. Mary Magdalen, which has a spire so tall, it looks like it's trying to poke the clouds. The church has been around since the 18th century, and it's all full of that old-world charm that makes you feel like you should be wearing a cravat, even if you're just there to take a selfie. There's a graveyard around the back, as there always is with old churches, filled with ancient tombstones that lean a bit to the side, like they're tired from standing up for centuries.

And of course, because it's Tetbury, there's also a Woolsack Race. Yes, that's right—a race where people run up and down a hill carrying sacks of wool, because apparently, they thought carrying heavy things for fun would be a good way to remember their woolly heritage. It's one of those bizarre British traditions that makes no sense, but everyone gets very excited about it anyway. It's like a cross between weightlifting and a historical re-enactment, but with more chances of tripping over.

So, Tetbury: it's old, it's posh, and it's got enough antiques to keep the past going for a few more centuries. It's the sort of town where you can buy a scone that's been handcrafted to perfection and then go look at a chair that's older than the United States. And if you keep an eye out, you might just spot a royal or two, or at least their gardener. It's got all the charm of the Cotswolds, wrapped up in a little bundle of history, luxury, and the occasional nod to a sheep.

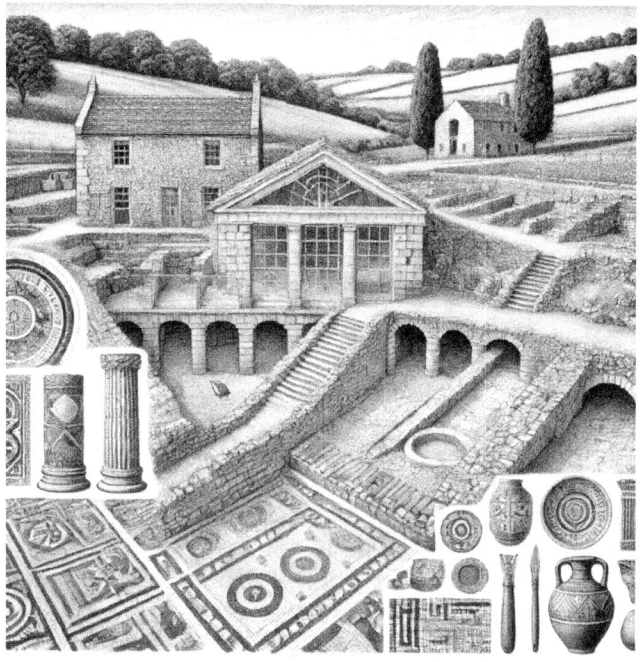

32 CHEDWORTH ROMAN VILLA

Chedworth Roman Villa. It sounds like it should be full of gladiators and people shouting in Latin, doesn't it? But actually, it's a Roman villa tucked away in the Cotswolds, where ancient Romans probably wandered around in togas, looking at the view and thinking, "Yes, I could do with a nice warm bath right now." Because back in Roman times, everyone seemed to be obsessed with baths. If you couldn't take a bath, you might as well have stayed home.

Chedworth is one of the biggest Roman villas in Britain, which means it's like the Buckingham Palace of ancient ruins, but with fewer guards and more bits of broken pottery. It was built around 120 AD, which is ages ago—so long ago that most of the people who lived there probably thought that throwing coins into a fountain could solve all their problems. It's set in a lovely little valley, surrounded by trees, like the Romans thought, "Let's build ourselves a luxury countryside retreat, but in Gloucestershire, because why not?"

Back then, Chedworth would have been the height of Roman luxury—like having an infinity pool, but with a lot more marble and mosaics. The villa had everything you could want in a 4th-century holiday home: fancy dining rooms, heated floors, and even a hypocaust system, which is basically Roman underfloor heating. It's where they'd light a fire underneath the floor, and the hot air would flow through the space, warming up the rooms. It's a bit like the Roman version of central heating, except with a lot more smoke and the constant risk of accidentally burning your foot.

The highlight of Chedworth Roman Villa has to be the mosaics. You know those pictures you make out of tiny squares at school? Well, the Romans did that, but on a scale that makes it look like they were trying to cover the entire planet in patterned floors. There's a mosaic of a little fish, which is nice if you're into fish, and then there are all these geometric designs that make you think the Romans spent way too much time thinking about triangles. They didn't even have television back then, so I guess designing floor art was the next best thing.

They also had a private bathhouse, because no self-respecting Roman would be caught dead without a proper place to have a soak. There's a cold plunge pool, a warm room, and a hot room, because the Romans had their bathing routine down to a science. It's like they invented the spa day, but instead of candles and essential oils, they had slaves chucking logs into the fire to keep the water nice and toasty. Imagine that—having a cold plunge just for the fun of it. These days, most of us wouldn't even bother with that if it came with a free Wi-Fi signal.

But of course, time wasn't too kind to Chedworth. After the Romans packed up and left Britain—probably because they'd had enough of the weather—the villa fell into ruin, like a Roman Airbnb that no one wanted to rent anymore. It just sat there for centuries, slowly falling apart, until a Victorian bloke named James Farrer turned up in 1864 and decided to dig it up. He was one of those "gentleman archaeologists," which is a polite way of saying he was rich, bored, and didn't mind getting his hands dirty. And lucky for us, he did, because now we've got this lovely pile of stones to look at and think, "Wow, the Romans really knew how to make a nice floor."

Today, Chedworth Roman Villa is run by the National Trust, which means you can visit it, wander around the ruins, and try to imagine what it was like when it wasn't just a bunch of foundations and walls. There's a little museum with all sorts of Roman bits and bobs, like coins, pottery, and some old shoes that make you realize that footwear really hasn't improved that much in 2,000 years. And they've even put a modern roof over part of the villa to keep the weather off the mosaics, which is ironic when you think about how the Romans had to put up with British rain without a single raincoat.

There's also this lovely little spring that bubbles up on the site, which the Romans probably thought was magical, because back then, if water came out of the ground, it was either a gift from the gods or a good place to chuck in a few offerings and hope for the best. They built a nymphaeum over it, which is basically a posh way of saying "water shrine," and they'd leave little offerings to the water nymphs, probably hoping they'd get good luck or at least a nice bath out of it.

So, Chedworth Roman Villa: it's ancient, it's mysterious, and it's got more intricate floor designs than you'd know what to do with. It's the sort of place that makes you think, "Wow, the Romans really knew how to live," even if that life involved a lot of cold rooms, strange rituals, and a general lack of central plumbing. It's a bit of the ancient world tucked away in the English countryside, reminding us that even 2,000 years ago, people liked a bit of luxury—and a good soak. And honestly, who can blame them?

Chedworth Roman Villa: Yanworth, Near Cheltenham, Gloucestershire, GL54 3LJ. www.nationaltrust.org.uk/visit/gloucestershire-cotswolds/chedworth-roman-villa

33 COTSWOLDS WILDLIFE PARK

Cotswold Wildlife Park. That's a place that sounds like it should be full of sheep and maybe a very posh pheasant, doesn't it? Like a park where you wander around, nodding at different types of hedgerows and pretending you know what an otter looks like in the wild. But no—this place is so much more. It's like a little slice of the Serengeti, except it's in the Cotswolds, where people still get excited about a nice bit of dry stone walling.

The park's just outside Burford, in the middle of the Cotswolds, and it's got over 160 acres of animals, which is basically a fancy way of saying, "We've got loads of space and we've filled it with as many creatures as possible." And not just the usual British stuff like badgers and foxes, but proper exotic animals like giraffes, lions, and penguins, which are definitely not native to Gloucestershire. It's like they've taken the concept of a zoo and given it a nice country house makeover, like a zebra might come round with a tray of scones if you're lucky.

The park itself is set around this lovely old manor house, which makes you feel like you've stumbled into the stately home of someone who thought, "You know what would look great on the lawn? A rhino." And there *are* rhinos, just wandering around the grounds, looking like they belong there, even though they're about as far from the African savannah as you can get. It's all very quaintly British, having tea in the shadow of a grazing white rhino, as if that's just a normal Tuesday.

One of the best bits is the giraffe enclosure, because it's right in front of the manor house, and seeing giraffes poking their heads up against a backdrop of classic English architecture is a bit surreal, like you've walked into a very elaborate joke about colonialism. The giraffes look down on everyone, which must make them feel quite superior, especially since they've got the best view in the whole park.

And then there's the lemur walk-through, which is exactly what it sounds like—a place where you can stroll around while lemurs jump around like they own the place. They're not behind bars or anything, they're just there, eyeing you up as if they're deciding whether or not you're worth stealing a snack from. It's like being in a nature documentary, except instead of David Attenborough's soothing voice, you've got your own kids shouting, "Look, Mum, it's doing a dance!"

The park's also got penguins, because apparently, someone

thought, "What's missing from this corner of the English countryside? I know—penguins!" They've got their own little pool, and they do that cute waddle that makes everyone go, "Aww," even though in real life, they probably wouldn't last five minutes if they had to make their way across a muddy field in the Cotswolds.

They've got lions too, but don't worry—they're in a proper enclosure, not just wandering around the gardens scaring the peacocks. It's like a mini safari, but with more overcast skies and a tea room nearby. And if you've ever wanted to see a meerkat standing on a rock, looking suspiciously like it's waiting for a film crew, this is definitely the place to do it.

There's a lot of birds as well—owls, flamingos, parrots, you name it. And they've even got a train that you can ride around the park on, because nothing says "exotic wildlife experience" like chugging past the camels in a little red train while eating an ice cream. It's got that family-day-out vibe where you can pretend you're doing something educational, even if you're really just trying to spot which animal has the silliest face.

And because this is the Cotswolds, it's all very picturesque. There are walled gardens and lovely flower beds, so you can feel like you're in a period drama, except with more monkeys. You can walk through a Victorian greenhouse full of exotic plants and pretend you're an explorer discovering a new species, when really you're just hoping the butterfly house doesn't make you too sweaty.

The Cotswold Wildlife Park is one of those places where you get a bit of everything—zebras on a lawn, lemurs doing their best impression of escape artists, and lions that look like they're slightly disappointed with the British weather. It's a weird and wonderful mix of safari adventure and a day out at your nan's favourite garden centre. It's perfect for a bit of escapism, even if you do have to put up with the occasional drizzle.

So, Cotswold Wildlife Park: it's not just a place for animals, it's a place where you can feel like you're seeing the wonders of the world without actually leaving the comfort of Gloucestershire. It's like someone decided that all of nature should be available for viewing within an hour's drive of a cream tea, and honestly, who can argue with that?

Cotswold Wildlife Park: Bradwell Grove, Burford, Oxfordshire, OX18 4JP. www.cotswoldwildlifepark.co.uk

34 KELMSCOTT MANOR

Kelmscott Manor. One of those places that sounds like it should come with its own haunted attic and a butler called Jeeves, doesn't it? But actually, it's a beautiful old farmhouse in the middle of the Oxfordshire countryside that's got more art history than you can shake a paisley scarf at. It's most famous for being the country home of William Morris, who was this Victorian bloke that did absolutely everything—he was a designer, a poet, a socialist, a furniture-maker, and probably would have been an influencer if they'd had Instagram back then.

The house dates back to the 17th century, which means it's properly old, even by British standards. It's all made out of that lovely grey Cotswold stone that makes everything look like it's been smoothed over by time and just a bit of drizzle. The whole place looks like a postcard you'd buy at a National Trust gift shop, with its thatched roof, ivy-covered walls, and a garden that's so perfectly overgrown, it's like nature and the gardeners had a bit of an argument but then decided to compromise.

When William Morris found Kelmscott Manor, he thought he'd discovered the perfect escape from all the noise and dirt of London. And to be fair, if you were living in Victorian London with all the smog and people shouting about horse manure in the streets, you'd probably want a nice peaceful manor house too. He called it "heaven on earth," which is a bit over the top, but that's Morris for you—he liked to wax lyrical about everything, from wallpaper to the way a chair leg curves.

Morris used Kelmscott Manor as his country retreat, where he could sit around thinking deep thoughts and being very serious about how terrible the industrial revolution was. He believed in beautiful things and craftsmanship, which is a fancy way of saying he thought everything should look pretty and be made by someone who knew what they were doing. He and his mates from the Pre-Raphaelite Brotherhood would come here to hang out and talk about art and probably complain about how modern life was ruining everything. They were like the original hipsters, but with more medieval-inspired robes.

Inside, the house is crammed full of Morris's designs—fancy tapestries, intricate wallpapers, and furniture that looks like it belongs in a fairy tale. It's the kind of place where even the cushions have more artistic merit than most of us can muster in a lifetime. Everything's covered in those iconic floral patterns, the kind where you can't tell if you're looking at a beautiful rose or a slightly trippy fever dream. It's like stepping inside one of those old books about how nature is very inspiring, except instead of reading about it, you're sitting on it.

And of course, because it's William Morris, the whole place has a bit of a political vibe too. He was really into the idea that everyone should have access to beautiful things, which is a lovely thought, but a bit ironic when you realize that his wallpaper costs more than most people's rent these days. But let's not get bogged down in the details—he was all about art and beauty and the kind of socialist ideals that sound great when you're sitting in a garden with a cup of tea.

Speaking of gardens, Kelmscott's got a lovely one. It's a bit wild, which is exactly how Morris liked it—he thought gardens should look natural, like they just sort of happened on their own, even if they've secretly got a team of gardeners working hard behind the scenes. It's got flowers, orchards, and little paths that make you feel like you might bump into a woodland sprite if you take a wrong turn. It's the kind of garden that makes you think, "Yes, I should really get into gardening," before remembering that the closest you've come to that is overwatering a basil plant.

Nowadays, Kelmscott Manor is run by the Society of Antiquaries, which sounds like a bunch of very serious people in tweed, but really it just means you can visit and pretend you're as cultured as Morris and his mates. You can wander through the house, look at all the beautiful old stuff, and try to figure out which bits are original and which ones have been carefully restored to look old. There's a little café, too, because it wouldn't be a proper British heritage site without somewhere to get a scone and a cup of tea.

So, Kelmscott Manor: it's a little slice of Victorian idealism, wrapped up in medieval charm and a whole lot of floral patterns. It's the sort of place that makes you feel like you should start writing poetry or campaigning for a better world, but you'll probably just take a few nice photos and think about how lovely it would be to live in the countryside. It's got history, it's got art, and it's got enough William Morris designs to make you wonder why everything in your own home looks so boring. And really, isn't that what a visit to a manor house is all about? Feeling a bit inspired, a bit nostalgic, and a bit glad you don't have to deal with all that Victorian plumbing.

Kelmscott Manor: Kelmscott, Lechlade, Gloucestershire, GL7 3HJ. www.kelmscottmanor.org.uk

35 BICESTER SHOPPING VILLAGE

Bicester Shopping Village. A place that sounds like it should be a quaint little cluster of shops selling turnips and locally made wool socks, doesn't it? Like something you'd find in a sleepy English village where the biggest excitement is the church fete. But no—Bicester Village is the complete opposite of that. It's not really a village at all, it's more like a shopping theme park, where the main attraction is spending money on things you probably don't need, but they make you feel very fancy.

It's in a place called Bicester, which is pronounced like "Bister," because, for some reason, the English decided that certain letters are just there for decoration. And instead of being full of country charm, Bicester Village is full of luxury outlet shops, which is a posh way of saying "expensive stuff, but slightly cheaper than usual." It's the sort of place where people go to feel like they're getting a bargain, even though they're still paying more than they would for a normal pair of shoes.

They've got all the big designer names here—Gucci, Prada, Dior—basically all those brands that sound like they should come with a free sports car. And the whole place is laid out like a picturesque little street, except instead of a butcher and a greengrocer, you've got high-end boutiques selling handbags that cost more than your mortgage. Everything's designed to look like a perfect little village, with flower boxes, cobbled walkways, and nice, neat little shops, but let's be honest—no real village ever had this many people carrying designer shopping bags while sipping lattes.

It's like Disneyland for grown-ups, but instead of rides, you've got changing rooms, and instead of Mickey Mouse, you've got a personal shopper offering you cashmere sweaters. There's even a concierge service, which is basically a fancy word for "someone who will hold your bags while you continue to shop," because apparently that's a real need here. People come from all over the world to shop here, too—coaches pull in full of tourists, all hoping to find a pair of discounted designer trainers and a scarf that makes them feel like they're in a Vogue spread.

The restaurants and cafés at Bicester Village are all very nice, too—no greasy spoons here, no sir. It's more about having a leisurely lunch with a glass of champagne before heading back out to try on yet another pair of trousers. They've got a mix of fancy bistros, patisseries, and places that do avocado toast, because what's a luxury shopping experience without paying extra for a bit of green mush on bread? It's all about creating that feeling that you're not just shopping, you're living a lifestyle—one that just happens to involve carrying around a lot of bags.

And because this is England, they've tried to make the whole experience feel a bit historic, even though it's really just a bunch of shops on a mission to part you from your money. They've added little touches, like fake old-fashioned street signs and lots of greenery, so it's a bit like someone took a picture-perfect village and replaced all the residents with mannequins dressed in this season's must-haves.

But the real magic of Bicester Village is how it makes people feel like they're part of some exclusive club, even if that club is just full of people trying to find a designer handbag at a slight discount. It's like, for one day, you get to feel like you're living the high life, swanning around with your branded bags, even if you'll be eating beans on toast for the next month to pay off the credit card bill.

It's also brilliantly located—right near a train station, so you can hop straight off the train from London, step into the "village," and immediately start questioning whether you need a new pair of sunglasses, even though it's February and hasn't been sunny for weeks. It's like they knew exactly how to trap people with a disposable income who are looking for a reason to justify buying yet another designer coat.

So, Bicester Village: it's not a village, but it is a kind of fantasy land, where everyone pretends that paying slightly less for a pair of designer shoes is the deal of a lifetime. It's posh, it's polished, and it's definitely not what most people think of when they imagine a trip to the English countryside. But if you're after a day out that makes you feel like a celebrity on a shopping spree, then this is the place to be. Just don't ask too many questions about why there are no cows or quaint village pubs—there's no time for that when you're eyeing up the latest handbag.

Bicester Shopping Village: 50 Pingle Drive, Bicester, Oxfordshire, OX26 6WD. www.thebicestercollection.com

36 LONG COMPTON

Long Compton. A village name that sounds like it's trying very hard to make sure you know it's not just any old Compton—it's the *long* one. And it is long, in the sense that it's stretched out along the edge of the Cotswolds, with houses and cottages that seem to go on forever, like a village that's tried to make itself into a country lane but hasn't quite managed to stop. It's one of those places where time sort of meanders, like a slow walk with a dog that keeps stopping to sniff every hedge.

Long Compton's been around for ages—like, ancient ages. It's mentioned in the Domesday Book, which is basically the medieval equivalent of getting your name in the phone book, except with more talk about sheep and land ownership. People have been living here since before they even knew how to write things down, probably because it's got that classic English village charm—rolling hills, old stone cottages, and fields full of crops or sheep, depending on the time of year.

And speaking of ancient, Long Compton has this big, spooky legend that ties into the Rollright Stones, which are just up the road. Apparently, there's this old story that a witch cursed the village, saying that one day there'd be a king and his army marching through, but she'd turn them all to stone. Which, if you're the sort of person who believes in witches and their love of turning things into inanimate objects, sounds quite dramatic. So, the stones became the Rollright Stones, and the village kept going, probably thinking, "Well, at least she didn't turn us into rocks."

It's also got a church, St. Peter and St. Paul's, which is one of those classic English churches where every brick looks like it's seen a bit too much rain. It's got a graveyard full of old tombstones that lean at odd angles, like they're trying to gossip about the 17th century. And inside, there's medieval bits and pieces, stained glass windows, and that slightly cold, damp smell that's somehow comforting in a place where people have been praying for centuries. The church is like the village itself—quiet, old, and with a few secrets it's not planning on telling anytime soon.

But Long Compton isn't just about ancient history. It's a proper village with a pub, because you can't have an English village without a place to gather and talk about the weather. And there's a village shop, which is one of those places where you can buy milk, a lottery ticket, and have a chat with the person behind the counter who definitely knows everyone's business. It's the kind of place where, if you're new, people might wonder who you are and what you're doing there, but they'll still be polite about it because it's the countryside, and that's just what you do.

Long Compton's got that special Cotswold charm, where everything feels just a bit too perfect to be real—like you've wandered onto the set of a TV show about village life, and you half-expect a detective to turn up to solve a murder involving an old clockmaker and a missing pie recipe. But mostly, it's just very peaceful, with lots of green fields, hedgerows, and a sense that life's been going on here for a long time without needing to change much.

It's one of those places where people come to get away from it all and then realize there wasn't actually all that much to get away from in the first place. It's got charm, history, and a few mysteries about witches and stone circles, but it's also just a lovely, sleepy spot where the biggest excitement might be a tractor trundling through the high street.

So, Long Compton: it's old, it's quiet, and it's got just enough weird legends to keep things interesting. It's the kind of village where you can sit on a bench, look at the hills, and think, "Yes, this is exactly what I imagined the English countryside to be." Even if you're still not entirely sure why the witch turned everyone into rocks, but you're glad she decided to leave the village alone.

37 COTSWOLD WATER PARK

The Cotswold Water Park? Right, so it's not actually a water park like you'd expect—you know, with slides, wave pools, and kids running around in armbands. No, this is Britain, where we do things more mildly, understated and more sedate. It's just a lot of lakes. About 150 of them. Because apparently, if you dig up enough gravel, nature decides to fill in the holes with water and you get to call it a "water park."

It's basically what would happen if you gave the Cotswolds a bath and forgot to pull the plug. All those lakes were made by humans, so it's like Mother Nature didn't bother to show up, and people were like, "Fine, we'll do it ourselves." So now it's a place where you can go sailing, kayaking, or swimming if you fancy a dip in water that's probably just cold enough to give you mild regret.

And the name—Cotswold Water Park—is a bit misleading, isn't it? I mean, you hear "water park," and you think of water slides and lazy rivers. But instead, it's just a bunch of lakes where you do "activities." Which is another way of saying "outdoor things that will make you tired and a bit damp."

The wildlife is big here too. You've got birds, ducks, and the occasional fish that are probably living their best lives in these accidental lakes. It's also apparently a hot spot for birdwatchers, because if you're the kind of person who enjoys sitting still for hours waiting for a bird to show up, this place is basically Disneyland for you.

The whole area is huge—it covers loads of villages, so it's not like you can walk around it in a day unless you've got the stamina of a marathon runner or are very bad at reading maps. But there are lovely paths, pubs, and places to stay if you like your holidays to involve both "nature" and "lying down." There is even an inland sandy 'beach' with swimming lagoon at Shorncote. Pack your swimming costume, a 'kiss me quick' hat and pretend you're in Bognor. Just don't expect too much in the way of donkey rides, sticks of rock or candy floss.

In summary, the Cotswold Water Park is a clever way of turning gravel pits into something people will pay money to visit. It's very scenic, very relaxing, and very British in the sense that it's both pleasant and slightly underwhelming at the same time and often more than a bit cold and damp.

Cotswold Water Park: Visitor's Centre, Spine Road, South Cerney, Gloucestershire, GL7 5FP. www.waterpark.org

38 SLAD

Slad? Oh, right, that's a village, not a typo. Slad is a tiny place in the Cotswolds, and when I say tiny, I mean *blink and you'll miss it*. In fact, you could probably sneeze and accidentally drive through the whole village. But somehow, it's famous, mostly because of a man called Laurie Lee who wrote *Cider with Rosie*, which is basically a book about growing up in Slad. So, in a way, it's a whole village that became famous for being written about, which is quite clever when you think about it—if you're small and quiet enough, people start romanticizing you.

Laurie Lee described Slad as if it was some kind of rural paradise, but the reality is it's a place where nothing much happens, but that's kind of the point. It's all rolling hills, fields, and cows looking at you like you're the one who shouldn't be there. It's a postcard village, the sort of place where people go for long, thoughtful walks, usually wearing very expensive wellies they only bought for that one weekend and that are pinching their toes a bit.

There's a pub called The Woolpack, which is basically the village's social hub. It's where you go to imagine you're in a Laurie Lee novel or just to wonder why people still haven't invented pubs with Wi-Fi in villages like this. You can sit there with a pint of local cider and think about how quiet the world would be if no one had invented London.

Not much else happens in Slad. It's a place where time kind of stands still, which is perfect if you're into gazing wistfully at the countryside, imagining yourself in a BBC period drama, or just avoiding other people in general.

In conclusion, Slad is one of those villages where nothing happens but in a way that makes people write books about how magical it is. It's quaint, it's peaceful, and it's a great place to visit if your idea of excitement is spotting a sheep in the distance.

39 STROUD

Stroud? So, Stroud is like the rebellious teenager of the Cotswolds. You've got all these pretty, posh villages with their tea rooms and antique shops, and then there's Stroud, which is more like, "Nah, we're doing our own thing, mate." It's a bit scruffier, a bit more alternative—like the Cotswolds discovered tie-dye and indie music and just went with it.

Stroud's famous for its markets, and not just any markets— *farmers' markets*. Which is where people who have never farmed a day in their life go to buy vegetables that still have dirt on them. It's like paying extra for nature to remind you that carrots come from the ground, not a supermarket shelf. It's all very organic and wholesome, which is great if you love the idea of spending £5 on a tomato.

The town's also a hotspot for artists and creatives. It's one of those places where everyone seems to be making something—pottery, paintings, artisanal bread—probably all at the same time. You can't walk five minutes without stumbling into an art gallery or some pop-up exhibition of "found objects," which, to the rest of us, just looks like stuff they found in a skip.

Stroud is big on community, which means loads of people doing things together, like yoga in the park or protesting about stuff like plastic straws up the noses of turtles and global warming. There's always some sort of cause people are passionate about, and it's very eco-friendly. It's the kind of place where if you accidentally use a plastic bag, someone will politely but firmly explain why you're the problem with the world.

Then there's the countryside around Stroud—it's gorgeous. But instead of just looking at it, people here like to be *in* it. They're all about walking, cycling, and hugging trees. Probably. The views are stunning, and it's like the hills are just there to remind you that you should've gone to the gym more.

So, in summary, Stroud is like the cool, artsy cousin of the Cotswolds. It's got the charm, but with a side of rebellion, as if someone decided to stick a festival inside a market town and never told the residents it was over. If you like your organic veg with a side of activism and your art a bit confusing, you'll fit right in.

40 PAINSWICK

Painswick? Basically, it's another one of those Cotswold villages that sounds like it should be a fancy type of cheese, doesn't it? But no, it's a real place, and it's often called "The Queen of the Cotswolds," which is ironic, because it's a village, not a person. You can't make a village a queen, but apparently, Painswick thought, "Why not?"

The village is all honey-coloured stone buildings and quaint little streets, like someone designed it specifically to be on a jigsaw puzzle. It's the kind of place where nothing much happens, but it's so pretty that people come here just to walk around and feel anxious about how much more picturesque it is than where they live.

The big thing in Painswick is the yew trees in the churchyard. Now, I'm not saying Painswick is obsessed with its yew trees, but they've got 99 of them, and apparently, there's some legend that says if they ever plant a 100th tree, the devil will come and, I don't know, ruin the village fête or something. It's one of those weird superstitions people in pretty villages come up with to make life sound a bit more exciting than it actually is.

The church itself, St Mary's, is quite famous too. It's all Gothic and pointy, like churches are, but the real attraction is those trees—because nothing says "come visit" like a load of perfectly trimmed bushes. They even have a yew tree trimming festival, which is basically an excuse to celebrate topiary. I mean, who wouldn't want to throw a party about cutting shrubs into shapes?

Painswick Beacon is another thing. It's a big hill you can walk up, which, to be honest, sounds exhausting. But apparently, you get great views from the top, so it's worth it if you like standing on a windy hill feeling superior to the people in the valley below.

In summary, Painswick is like the Cotswolds on steroids. It's got everything—cute stone cottages, a spooky churchyard, and a lot of trees that people are oddly protective of. If you want a village that feels like it's constantly auditioning to be in a Jane Austen adaptation, Painswick's your place. Just don't ask for a 100th yew tree, or you might summon the devil and ruin someone's cream tea.

41 HIDCOTE HOUSE AND GARDENS

Hidcote House and Gardens? Oh, that's one of those fancy National Trust places where everything looks like it's been perfectly arranged by a gardening god who probably whispers Latin plant names in their sleep. It's one of the most famous gardens in the UK, but, let's be honest, it's mainly famous because it's big and full of plants.

Hidcote was created by some bloke called Lawrence Johnston, who clearly didn't know when to stop planting things. He was one of those gardening obsessives who probably saw a patch of dirt and thought, "Not on my watch!" and then immediately filled it with flowers. Apparently, Johnston was American, which is surprising, because the garden looks as British as a cup of tea served by a butler in a bowler hat.

Now, the clever bit about Hidcote is that it's made up of a bunch of little "garden rooms." Yes, *rooms*. Because apparently, normal gardens weren't posh enough, so Johnston decided to divide his garden into sections like it's a botanical real estate agency. You've got the "White Garden," the "Red Border," and the "Fuchsia Garden," all very creative names. It's basically a garden that's had a lot of interior design ideas thrown at it.

Hidcote is known for its "Arts and Crafts" style, which, if you don't know, was this whole movement where people decided to make things look old-fashioned and homemade, even though they weren't. It's like when you buy furniture that's been distressed on purpose—it's supposed to look like it's been through a lot, but really, it's brand new and just pretending to be interesting.

The whole place is very picturesque, perfect for people who like wandering around, pointing at plants and pretending they know what they're called. It's also full of little paths and secret nooks, so you can wander for hours without actually understanding where you are, which is great if you enjoy getting lost in a hedge maze without the maze part.

In conclusion, Hidcote House and Gardens is basically a very well-organised bit of nature, curated like an Instagram feed but with more dirt. If you like gardens that make you feel like a professional horticulturist even though you've only ever managed to keep a cactus alive, this is the spot for you. Plus, you get to say you've visited a garden that's so fancy it has "rooms"—which is the ultimate power move in the plant world.

Hidcote House and Gardens: Hidcote Bartrim, Near Chipping Campden, Gloucestershire, GL55 6LR.

www.nationaltrust.org.uk/visit/gloucestershire-cotswolds/hidcote

42 COTSWOLDS FALCONRY CENTRE

The Cotswold Falconry Centre? Right, so this is a place where birds of prey get to show off while humans stand around looking impressed. It's basically a talent show for eagles, owls, and falcons, except the judges are tourists who've paid money to watch birds do what they'd normally do for free—fly around and eat stuff.

It's got all these majestic birds like falcons, which are the ones that fly super fast, and eagles, which are basically the muscle-bound superheroes of the bird world. And then there are the owls, who look wise but are probably just thinking about mice the whole time. They do these flying displays where the birds swoop right over your head like they've got somewhere very important to be, but really, they're just hoping someone will throw them a dead chick or something.

The falconers who run the place act like they're bird whisperers, which is impressive, but let's be honest, they've basically trained the birds to show off for snacks. It's the bird equivalent of giving your dog a treat for sitting down, except these birds can fly at 200 miles an hour, which is slightly more impressive than your Labrador doing a half-hearted "paw."

And if you're into nature, or you just like the idea of a bird staring at you with a look that says, "I could eat you if I wanted to," then you'll love it. There's something thrilling about being so close to a bird that could probably take out your sandwich if it fancied.

In summary, the Cotswold Falconry Centre is a place where birds of prey get to be the stars of the show, while humans look on and pretend they're not a little bit scared. It's educational, it's thrilling, and it's a great reminder that, no matter how impressive we think we are as humans, we'll never look as cool as an eagle in full swoop mode.

Cotswold Falconry Centre: Batsford, Moreton in Marsh, Gloucestershire, GL56 9AT. www.cotswold-falconry.co.uk

43 SNOWHILL MANOR

Snowhill Manor? Oh, right, that's one of those places where someone got very rich, very eccentric, and then decided to fill their house with a lot of *stuff*. Like, so much stuff that the house isn't so much a home as it is a museum of "Why did you buy that?"

The guy behind it all was Charles Wade, who wasn't content with having one of those lovely Cotswold homes with a few tasteful antiques. No, he decided to cram every corner of Snowshill Manor with an overwhelming collection of weird and wonderful objects—like armour, musical instruments, toys, bicycles, and... random bits of junk. Imagine being so into collecting things that your house becomes a glorified storage unit, except with more Tudor furniture.

Wade didn't even *live* in the manor house itself. He just used it to show off his hoard of curiosities while he lived in a tiny cottage next door, which is the kind of bonkers move that makes you wonder if he thought his collection might get annoyed with him. "No, I can't live amongst all those samurai swords—I might bump into one while reaching for my slippers."

The house is full of rooms with names like the "Green Room" and the "Room of Toys," which sounds innocent until you realise it's full of slightly creepy, old-fashioned toys that look like they might come to life at night and start plotting. Wade was clearly fascinated by the weird and wonderful, and by "fascinated," I mean "probably spent far too much time on eBay if it had existed back then."

The gardens are pretty nice too, though Wade wasn't as obsessed with plants as he was with random objects. They're designed like outdoor rooms—because apparently, back then, people were obsessed with the idea of turning everything into "rooms," even the bits with grass and flowers.

In summary, Snowshill Manor is a house that's less about living and more about hoarding, but in a classy, National Trust kind of way. It's perfect for anyone who's ever thought, "I wish I had more unnecessary things in my life," or just wants to see what happens when a collector goes off the deep end. You'll leave feeling very grateful for your own minimalist Ikea setup, I can tell you that.

Snowshill Manor: Snowshill, Broadway, Worcestershire, WR12 7JU.
www.nationaltrust.org.uk/visit/gloucestershire-cotswolds/snowshill-manor-and-garden

44 THE FARMER'S DOG PUB (CLARKSON'S PUB)

Jeremy Clarkson's Farmer's Dog pub? Well, that's just about the most Jeremy Clarkson thing you could imagine, isn't it? Of course, he's gone and opened a pub. Because when you've driven every car on the planet, insulted half of it, and shouted at the other half, what else is left but to pull a pint and call it a day?

Now, I imagine Clarkson's pub isn't just any regular pub—it's probably a bit like him: loud, opinionated, and larger than life. It's called "The Farmer's Dog," which makes sense, because he's doing this whole farming thing now, isn't he? And when you

135

think about it, running a pub is just another way of farming—except instead of growing crops, you're growing people's ability to tolerate your opinions after a few pints.

I bet the pub's got a big sign outside, with a dog on it—probably a massive, no-nonsense working dog, like a sheepdog or something that looks like it could herd cows and insult you at the same time. Inside, it's probably all big wooden beams, leather chairs, and a roaring fire, because Clarkson's not the type to do anything by halves. It's probably got a menu full of hearty British food, but you just know it'll be written in some overly masculine way, like "MASSIVE STEAK" or "BLOKE'S PIE"—as if eating anything smaller than a tractor would damage your dignity.

And let's be honest, the beer's probably got his name on it. Clarkson's Craft Ale or something, brewed with hops that he's driven over in a Lamborghini tractor. You can just picture it: every pint comes with a side of automotive trivia and a rant about health and safety regulations.

As for the atmosphere, well, it's probably a mix of farmers, locals, and Clarkson fans who've come to sip their pint and wait for him to turn up so they can ask him about *Top Gear*. If you're lucky, you might even get to hear him grumble about tractors or Brexit or whatever else is annoying him that day.

In conclusion, Jeremy Clarkson's Farmer's Dog pub is exactly what you'd expect from the man—big, bold, and unapologetically Clarkson. It's a place where you can enjoy a pint, some hearty food, and maybe even hear a rant about why electric cars are ruining the world. Because at the end of the day, it's not just a pub—it's Clarkson in pub form.

The Farmer's Dog: Asthall Barrow Roundabout, Burford, Oxfordshire, OX18 4HJ. www.thefarmersdogpub.com

45 HIGHGROVE HOUSE & GARDENS

Highgrove? Well, that's King Charles's garden, isn't it? Well, technically it's his house *and* garden, but let's be honest, it's really all about the garden. Because Charles—sorry, *King* Charles—loves nothing more than pottering about with his plants, probably whispering sweet nothings to his roses while wearing tweed.

It's his personal paradise, like if a royal family member got a bit bored of waving at people and decided to spend their time making flowerbeds look perfect. The thing is, Charles has been into organic gardening since before it was trendy, back when "organic" just meant "don't spray it with stuff that makes the bees angry." So now, Highgrove is like the eco-friendly garden version of Buckingham Palace. Except there's fewer crowns and more compost.

Apparently, the garden is full of these little "rooms," which sounds posh, but really it's just a fancy way of saying, "I put some hedges here to make it look like walls." It's like Charles thought, "What if I make my garden more like a house?" Which makes sense, because if you're going to spend that much time in a garden, it might as well have different sections so you can feel like you're going on an adventure between the rhododendrons.

And then there's the wildflower meadow. Because what's the point of having a massive royal estate if you can't pretend to be a shepherd from a 19th-century poem? Charles planted loads of wildflowers, probably thinking it was good for the bees—and because nothing says "I'm down to earth" like making a field look like it hasn't been mown since 1742.

But it's not all about the flowers. There's a lot of weird garden art too, like sculptures and statues that make you wonder if Charles was trying to make a point or if he just had some extra stone lying around. And there's even a *stumpery*. Yes, you heard that right—a *stumpery*. It's basically a pile of old tree stumps, but because it's Highgrove, it's been turned into some sort of royal art installation. Only a royal could get away with calling a pile of wood an important garden feature.

In summary, Highgrove is like King Charles's very personal playground, where he gets to practice being a green-thumbed monarch while occasionally chatting with a fern. It's posh, it's organic, and it's exactly what you'd expect from someone who's spent his whole life being one fancy garden party away from becoming a full-time horticulturist. If you like gardens that are more complicated than most people's houses, this is the place for you.

Highgrove House and Gardens: A433, Doughton, Tetbury, Gloucestershire, GL8 8TQ. www.highgrovegardens.com

46 COTSWOLDS MOTORING MUSEUM

The Cotswold Motoring Museum? Oh, that's basically a big shed full of cars, but because it's in the Cotswolds, they've made it sound fancy. You know, slap the word "Cotswold" on anything, and suddenly people think it's charming, even if it's just a bunch of old cars covered in dust. It's like the Cotswolds' version of a time capsule, except instead of digging up ancient treasures, it's full of rusty bumpers and hubcaps from when your granddad was still in short trousers.

It's got all sorts of vintage cars, motorbikes, and caravans— which is basically like a collection of things people used to get stuck behind on narrow roads before we invented bypasses. They call it a "motoring museum," but let's be honest, it's more like a nostalgia trip for people who still think the best car ever made was the Ford Anglia.

There's also this little car called Brum. Now, if you don't know Brum, let me explain—he's a tiny car that's somehow also a children's TV star. Because apparently, back in the day, British television looked at a car and thought, "What if we make this car have feelings and solve crimes?" So Brum's there in the museum, just sitting around, not solving any crimes now, because, well, it's a museum, and even sentient cars need a break.

The whole place is filled with motoring memorabilia—posters, petrol cans, and all the other things people used to need when cars were more likely to break down than actually get you anywhere. It's the sort of place where you'll hear someone say, "Oh, I used to have one of those," at least fifty times while walking around. And if you don't know much about cars, don't worry—you'll still enjoy it, because it turns out old cars are quite fun to look at, even if you don't understand why they were so bad at cornering.

In summary, the Cotswold Motoring Museum is like a history lesson for people who love cars but hate reading books. It's full of charmingly unreliable vehicles from the past and a tiny TV car who, if we're honest, should've probably been given his own spin-off detective series by now. If you're into motoring or just like looking at things that remind you how much better your car is today, it's the place for you.

Cotswold Motoring Museum: Bourton on the Water, Gloucestershire, GL54 2BY. www.cotswoldmotoringmuseum.co.uk

47 COTSWOLDS SCULPTURE PARK

The Cotswold Sculpture Park? Right, so this is where art meets nature—or more specifically, where someone decided to stick a load of sculptures in a field and call it a park. It's like a regular park, but with fewer swings and more bits of metal twisted into shapes that make you go, "Is that supposed to be a horse, or have I had too much coffee?"

Basically, it's an outdoor gallery, except without walls, which is handy because you can pretend you're there for the fresh air when really, you're just wondering why half the sculptures look like someone's GCSE art project that got a bit out of hand.

There's all sorts of stuff—abstract shapes, giant figures, and things that look like they're from another planet but are probably just called something like "Reflection of Time" or "Contemplation in Steel."

The great thing about the Cotswold Sculpture Park is that it's one of those places where you can feel really cultured, even if you don't have the faintest idea what the sculptures are about. You can just walk around nodding and saying things like "interesting use of space" or "it really speaks to me," while secretly thinking, "Why's that one got three heads?" It's art you can't get told off for touching because you'd need a ladder to reach most of it.

Apparently, the sculptures change all the time, so if you go back, you'll see something different—which is great if you didn't understand the first lot and fancy being confused by some new ones. And it's all set in this lovely bit of countryside, so even if you don't "get" the art, you can still enjoy pretending to be at one with nature while you walk past a giant metal squid or whatever.

In conclusion, the Cotswold Sculpture Park is perfect if you like the idea of art but don't want to be stuck inside a gallery with people who know what they're talking about. It's got sculptures, trees, and just enough weirdness to make you feel like you're being very sophisticated, even if you're secretly wondering if one of the sculptures was made by accident.

Cotswold Sculpture Park: The Paddocks, Somerford Keynes, Gloucestershire, GL7 6FE. www.cotswoldsculpturepark.co.uk

48 CHELTENHAM RACECOURSE

Cheltenham Racecourse? Right, that's basically where people go to watch horses run in circles while wearing the fanciest hats they own, even though the horses couldn't care less about fashion. It's one of the most famous racecourses in the world, which is impressive when you think about it, because at the end of the day, it's just some grass with fences on it and a load of people betting their mortgage away.

The big event is the Cheltenham Festival, which is like Glastonbury for people who are really into horses, money, and wearing tweed. Everyone dresses up like they're going to meet the Queen, even though they're just there to stand in the cold, holding binoculars, pretending to know which horse looks the fastest. But honestly, can anyone really tell? They all look fast to me—they're horses.

And then there's the *Gold Cup*. This is the race where people get *really* excited. It's like the Super Bowl of jumping over fences—except without the halftime show and more mud. Everyone gets incredibly emotional about it, even though the horses don't know they're racing for a cup. They probably think, "Why is everyone shouting? I just want my carrot."

Let's not forget the betting. Cheltenham Racecourse is the kind of place where people who haven't placed a bet all year suddenly become experts on horse racing. "Oh, I've got a feeling about this one," they'll say, like they've got some kind of psychic connection with the jockey. Then they lose all their money and go, "Well, it's the experience that counts." Spoiler alert: it's not.

And the atmosphere? Oh, it's intense. You've got thousands of people all yelling at horses, waving their betting slips around like they mean something, and acting like their best mates with the jockeys. It's like being at a football match but with less chanting and more tweed jackets. And probably fewer people throwing beer in the air—probably.

In conclusion, Cheltenham Racecourse is the place to be if you like horses, hats, and the occasional reckless gamble. It's British culture at its finest: dressing up in ridiculous outfits, losing money, and pretending to know what's going on—all while standing in a field watching horses run away from people for no apparent reason. Perfect.

Cheltenham Racecourse: Evesham Road, Cheltenham, Gloucestershire, GL50 4SH. www.thejockeyclub.co.uk/cheltenham/

49 THE COTSWOLDS WAY

The Cotswold Way? Just basically a really long walk, isn't it? It's 102 miles of countryside, which sounds lovely until you realise that means walking for several days straight. It's like someone took a lovely afternoon stroll and then just kept going... and going... and going. By the time you're done, you've probably seen every possible combination of fields, trees, and sheep that the Cotswolds has to offer.

It runs from Chipping Campden to Bath, which is quite ambitious, really. I mean, most people struggle to walk to the shops without complaining, but here you're expected to march through 102 miles of rolling hills like it's some sort of medieval pilgrimage. Except instead of visiting a holy site, you're just hoping for a nice pub at the end of the day where they serve chips and real ale.

The Cotswold Way is all about those famous "honey-coloured" villages, which is just a posh way of saying "old stone buildings that look like they've been on every jigsaw puzzle ever." You walk through them, pretending you're in a period drama, and by day three, you're convinced you've seen the exact same pub and church ten times, just rearranged in different ways.

The views are spectacular, though, or at least people say they are. Lots of big hills and green fields, which are great for Instagram photos, but also a bit of a pain when you realise you've got to climb all the way to the top. And every time you think, "That must be the last hill," there's another one, waiting to ambush your legs.

And let's not forget the wildlife. You'll probably see some sheep, maybe a few cows, and if you're lucky, a bird that you can point at and say, "Look, nature." It's the kind of place where people feel obliged to be impressed by things they don't understand, like wildflowers. "Oh, look, a flower growing in a field—how rare!" Except it's not rare. It's just a field doing what fields do.

In summary, the Cotswold Way is perfect if you like walking for days on end through picturesque countryside while pretending you're the kind of person who enjoys walking for days on end through picturesque countryside. It's beautiful, exhausting, and by the time you've finished, you'll either be smug and at one with nature, or one step away from giving up on hiking altogether and taking up telly-viewing and heavy drinking.

50 CROCODILES OF THE WORLD

Crocodiles of the World? In the Cotswolds? That's just… confusing. You go to the Cotswolds expecting cottages, tea rooms, and the odd sheep. And then suddenly, bam—crocodiles. It's like someone looked at all that gentle, rolling countryside and thought, "You know what this place needs? Something that could bite your leg off."

Apparently, it's the UK's only crocodile zoo, which makes sense because I can't imagine there's a huge demand for crocs in Gloucestershire. But here it is, this entire place dedicated to creatures that look like they've just stepped out of the Jurassic period and into a sleepy bit of England where the most dangerous thing should be an angry badger.

So, they've got all sorts of crocodiles here—big ones, small ones, ones that are probably planning your demise the minute you turn your back. They also have alligators and caimans, which are basically crocodiles with slightly different accents. But let's be honest, unless you're a reptile expert, they all just look like really angry handbags with teeth.

There's a place where you can watch them being fed, which sounds exciting until you realise that crocodiles don't exactly do much apart from lurk in the water looking like they're planning world domination. And when they do move, it's either terrifyingly fast or painfully slow—there's no in-between. One minute they're sitting there like garden ornaments, the next they're snapping up some chicken like it's their last meal. It's basically the animal equivalent of someone who's always angry but can't be bothered to show it most of the time.

And if you're really into crocs, you can even hold a baby one. You know, for when you want the thrill of a potential mauling but in a safe, tiny package. It's cute in the way that all things that could kill you but haven't yet are cute.

In conclusion, Crocodiles of the World is one of the most bizarre things you'll find in the Cotswolds. It's like someone dropped a bit of the Amazon rainforest into middle England and decided to charge people for the privilege of being slightly nervous for a few hours. If you've ever wondered what it would be like to see a crocodile while also being within spitting distance of a cream tea, look no further!

Crocodiles of the World: Burford Road, Brize Norton, Oxfordshire, OX18 3NX. www.crocodilesoftheworld.co.uk

51 COTSWOLDS LAVENDER

Cotswold Lavender? It's a farm where they've decided to grow an entire field of lavender, because apparently, one or two lavender plants just weren't enough for them. No, they thought, "Let's fill acres of land with this stuff and watch people flock to take photos of it like it's some sort of purple paradise or Notre Dame."

So, it's basically a big field that smells like a soap shop or an old lady's knicker drawer, which people love. They wander around sniffing the air, like they've just discovered what scent is for the first time. And lavender—well, it's a plant that's mostly famous for making things smell "nice" in an old lady kind of way. You know, that scent you associate with your nan's wardrobe or those sachets people put in drawers because they think it'll keep their socks fresh.

But at Cotswold Lavender, it's not just about looking at and smelling the flowers—you can buy lavender in all sorts of forms. Lavender oil, lavender soap, lavender biscuits—because apparently, nothing says "delicious" like putting a flower known for its calming properties into your snack. I mean, who decided that was a good idea? "Oh, I love the smell of this plant, let's eat it too!" It's the edible equivalent of potpourri. They probably do lavender loo roll to make your bum smell fresh too!

And there's a gift shop, obviously. Because what would a field of lavender be without a place where you can spend far too much money on things you'll forget you bought? They've got lavender-themed everything—candles, creams, probably even lavender-themed lavender. It's all very soothing and gentle, which makes sense, because lavender's main job in life seems to be calming people down, even though most of them have never been that stressed to begin with.

The fields themselves look quite impressive in summer—rows and rows of purple stretching out into the distance, which is basically Instagram heaven. People take photos like they're in some sort of fairy tale, even though they're really just standing in a field full of bees that are having the time of their lives. It seems that lavender is basically catnip for bees.

In conclusion, Cotswold Lavender is where you go if you want to feel relaxed, smell like a drawer full of freshly ironed pants, and take photos that make it look like you've wandered into some sort of magical purple land. It's lavender, but more of it than you've ever needed, and somehow, that's exactly why it's so great!

Cotswold Lavender: Hill Barn Farm, Snowshill, Broadway, Worcestershire, WR12 7JY. www.cotswoldlavender.co.uk

52 CHRISTMAS IN THE COTSWOLDS

Christmas in the Cotswolds? That's like walking into a Christmas card that's been brought to life. It's all twinkling lights, ancient stone cottages covered in a light dusting of snow—if you're lucky—and people wandering around pretending to enjoy the cold because it's "festive." It's the sort of place where you half expect to see a Victorian carol singer pop out from behind a hedgerow, warbling *Deck the Halls* while someone hands you a mince pie you didn't ask for.

The villages go all out for Christmas, like they're competing to see who can look the most like a scene from *A Christmas Carol*. You've got places like Bourton-on-the-Water, where they stick a Christmas tree right in the middle of the river. Because, obviously, that's the best place for a tree—in water. Very practical. But people love it! They all stand around, sipping mulled wine, taking photos of it like it's the eighth wonder of the world, even though it's just a tree with some lights on, getting a bit soggy.

Then there's the Christmas markets. You've got to have a Christmas market these days. They pop up everywhere, like festive mushrooms. You wander around looking at stalls selling handmade candles and overpriced chutney, pretending you might buy something, but really just using it as an excuse to drink more mulled wine. You can't go five minutes without someone offering you something cinnamon-flavoured, because apparently, Christmas doesn't happen unless everything smells like a spice rack exploded.

Of course, there's also the traditional pub experience. Christmas in the Cotswolds isn't complete without sitting by an open fire in a 500-year-old pub, where the decorations look like they've been there since Henry VIII was on the throne. You'll be drinking something called "festive ale," which is just regular ale but with a picture of Santa on the pump, and your dog (because of course you've brought your dog) will be lying by the fire, probably wondering why humans get so weird in December.

And if you're really committed to the full-on Christmas experience, you've got to visit Blenheim Palace. They go absolutely bonkers with the lights. It's like someone handed them the National Grid and said, "Go on, use all of it." There's light trails, festive displays, and more decorations than Santa's grotto on steroids. You walk around, marvelling at how many lights they've managed to fit onto one building, and you can't help but think, "That's going to be one hell of an electricity bill."

In conclusion, Christmas in the Cotswolds is a mix of old-world charm and over-the-top festivities. It's all about pretending the cold is "cosy," drinking your body weight in mulled wine, and taking photos of things covered in fairy lights. It's magical, it's a bit ridiculous, and it's everything you never knew you needed from a very British Christmas.

53 COTSWOLDS FOOD AND DRINK

Dining out in the Cotswolds? It's an experience, isn't it? It's like the Cotswolds looked at regular food and thought, "How can we make this fancier and charge more for it?" Everything here is "local," "seasonal," and "organic," which basically means it's the same food as everywhere else, but it's been grown within a 10-mile radius and probably had a happier life than you.

The menus in Cotswold restaurants read like they were written by someone who thinks vegetables have feelings. You don't just get "carrots," do you? No, it's "heritage carrots, lovingly braised in Cotswold butter." Like the carrots have been personally massaged by the chef. And then there's "hand-dived scallops." I mean, does anyone really care *how* the scallops got here as long as they're on your plate?

And of course, the Cotswolds is famous for its gastropubs. It's not enough to just have a pub anymore—now it's got to be a *gastropub*. That's code for a place where you'll pay £25 for a pie and still leave hungry. The pub's probably 500 years old, with a thatched roof, an open fire, and furniture that looks like it's been there since the Middle Ages. You'll be sitting in a chair that's technically an antique, eating something called "foraged wild garlic soup," because apparently, they found the garlic in a forest and thought that was impressive enough to put on the menu.

Then there's the whole "farm to table" trend, which is just a fancy way of saying, "We got this from a farm nearby." Well, of course you did! It's the Cotswolds! Everything's nearby. You can't drive two minutes without running into a farm or a field full of sheep that probably have names and regular spa days.

And let's talk about afternoon tea. You can't come to the Cotswolds and not have afternoon tea. It's basically a law. You'll sit there in a quaint tearoom, nibbling on tiny sandwiches and scones, pretending it's completely normal to have cake at 3 p.m. while sipping tea out of a cup so small, it looks like it was made for a doll. But it's "charming" and "quaint," so no one questions why you've paid £30 to eat half a cucumber sandwich with a cup of weak tea.

In conclusion, dining out in the Cotswolds is a mix of fancy descriptions, old buildings, and food that's had more care and attention than most people's elderly parents. You'll leave feeling cultured, a bit poorer, and probably wondering why the potatoes tasted better just because they came from a field down the road. But that's the magic of the Cotswolds—everything is just a bit posher, including your dinner.

54 COTSWOLDS DISTILLERY

The Cotswolds Distillery is like the Buckingham Palace of booze – grand, British, and capable of making you feel a bit wobbly. Nestled in the heart of the Cotswolds, which is basically England's answer to a posh postcard, it's a place where they take simple ingredients, wave some sort of alchemical wand over them, and turn them into liquid happiness.

Their most famous creation is the Cotswolds Cloudy Gin, which isn't just gin—it's magic gin. Why? Because when you add tonic to it, it turns cloudy. That's right, cloudy! It's like a science experiment, but instead of learning something boring about atoms, you end up with a fancy cocktail. The cloudiness comes from essential oils in the botanicals, which they don't filter out because apparently, that's where all the flavour lives. So, if your gin goes cloudy, don't panic—it's not broken; it's just showing off.

But it's not all gin. Oh no, the Cotswolds Distillery also makes malt whisky that's so good, it could probably convince Scotland to hand over its crown. Their whisky is aged in barrels—fancy barrels, mind you, like ones that used to hold sherry or red wine. Apparently, this makes it taste richer, although honestly, if it's whisky, I'm just glad it doesn't taste like regret. Their single malt has won loads of awards, which means experts have sipped it and gone, "Yes, this is posh enough for us."

And then there are the liqueurs. They've got things like Cotswolds Cream Liqueur, which is basically dessert in a glass. It's like drinking a pudding, but no one judges you because it's got alcohol in it, so suddenly it's sophisticated. They also make other flavoured liqueurs, which are perfect for people who want to feel fancy but secretly just like things that taste like sweets.

The distillery itself is a proper destination. You can visit for a tour, which is basically an excuse to wander around shiny copper stills while someone tells you facts about booze. By the end of it, you'll know things like what botanicals are, how whisky gets its colour, and why barrels are so important—all of which you'll promptly forget after the tasting session. Speaking of which, they give you a chance to sample everything, which is both educational and a bit dangerous if you've skipped lunch.

There's even a shop where you can buy the spirits, along with other fancy things like glasses and cocktail books. It's the sort of place where you tell yourself, "I'm buying this as a gift," but then you end up drinking it yourself while watching reruns of Antiques

Roadshow.

In short, the Cotswolds Distillery is a wonderland for anyone who likes their drinks to taste great and come with a side of countryside charm. Whether it's their famous cloudy gin, award-winning whisky, or indulgent liqueurs, it's proof that the Cotswolds isn't just about sheep and cottages—it's also about getting merry in the most sophisticated way possible.

Cotswolds Distillery: Phillip's Field, Whichford Road, Stourton, Shipston on Stour, Warwickshire, CV36 5EX. www.cotswoldsdistillery.com

55 HOOK NORTON BREWERY

Ah, Hook Norton Brewery. It's not just a brewery; it's like a big, drunken church to beer. Located in the heart of the Cotswolds, it's one of the last surviving Victorian tower breweries in the UK, which is basically like saying it's the Stonehenge of beer-making but with fewer druids and more yeast.

The brewery itself looks like it's auditioning for the role of "quaintest building ever." It's a Victorian tower brewery, which means it's tall, old, and designed to use gravity to make beer. Yes, gravity—the same thing that keeps apples on trees and trousers on the floor after too many pints. This architectural masterpiece was built in 1899 and stands like a majestic castle of suds. Each floor in the tower is responsible for a different part of the brewing process. The malt starts at the top, then works its way down. So, the beer is literally brewed by falling. That's clever. Like a drunken waterfall.

It also has a steam engine, still functional today. That's right— Hook Norton doesn't just make beer; it also has its own steampunk aesthetic. This engine is used to power parts of the brewing process. It's like Willy Wonka's chocolate factory but less creepy and with more hops.

Now, let's talk about the brewery's dray horses. These massive Shire horses are like four-legged beer delivery trucks but much slower and with more personality. These big lads have been delivering beer to local pubs since before Deliveroo existed, proving once again that the old ways are often the best. And frankly, what's cooler than getting your pint delivered by a horse? A drone could never.

The horses are not just for show; they're living, breathing ambassadors for the brewery. They trot around the village and the surrounding areas, spreading the good word of Hook Norton beer, which is probably why the locals seem so cheerful.

Hook Norton makes a range of beers that cover all the important categories:

Milds: For when you want a beer that whispers instead of shouts.

Bitters: Proper traditional ales that taste like the word "pub" feels.

Seasonal Brews: These are beers they brew for a short time each year, like limited-edition trainers, but for your mouth.

Their flagship beer is Hooky, a light ale with enough character to make you consider naming your dog after it. Then there's Old Hooky, a stronger, darker beer that tastes like it could solve most of life's problems if given enough time. They also have more adventurous beers like Double Stout, which isn't just a stout; it's DOUBLE stout. Twice the stoutness. That's science.

And let's not forget their IPAs and pale ales, which are crafted for those who think beer should taste like a field of hops slapped you in the face, in a good way.

Visiting Hook Norton Brewery is like going to a museum, but instead of looking at old things and pretending to be interested, you actually get beer. You can tour the brewery, meet the horses, and sample the beers. It's basically a perfect day out, unless you don't like beer, horses, or fun.

Hook Norton Brewery isn't just a place where beer is made; it's a living, breathing monument to everything good about British drinking culture. The architecture is stunning, the horses are massive, and the beer is delicious. If it were any more British, it would sing "God Save the King" every time you ordered a pint. In summary: it's history, hops, and horses. What more could you want?

Hook Norton Brewery: Brewery Lane, Hook Norton, Oxfordshire, OX15 5NY. www.hooky.co.uk

56 THE BIG FEASTIVAL

The Big Feastival is like a music festival that went to Waitrose, bought a load of fancy snacks, and decided to settle down in the Cotswolds. It's held every summer on Alex James's farm. Yes, that's *the* Alex James—the bloke from Blur who used to write songs about park life and now writes songs about parmesan. He's swapped Britpop for brie, and honestly, who wouldn't?

At the heart of it all is Alex's Cheese Hub. It's basically a giant shrine to dairy, with all his fancy cheeses on display. He makes things like "Blue Monday," which is a blue cheese but without the sad bits, and "Goddess," which sounds like it should come with a crown but is actually just ridiculously creamy. The Cheese Hub is the place to be—it's got cheese, drinks, and occasionally Alex himself, hanging about like a rock-star cheesemonger. Imagine getting your cheddar served by the bloke who wrote Song 2. That's what they call an experience.

But the Big Feastival isn't just about cheese (although, to be honest, it should be). It's got everything: live music, food trucks, and enough activities for kids to make them forget that their parents are spending the family holiday budget on pulled pork and craft gin. The music lineup is always a mix of nostalgic bands, chart-toppers, and the sort of acts you'd hear in the background at John Lewis. It's not the edgy type of festival where everyone's rolling in mud—it's the sort of festival where people bring deckchairs and Instagram their avocado toast.

The food is next level. They've got Michelin-starred chefs doing demonstrations, street food stalls selling things you can't pronounce, and enough free samples to technically call it lunch. And because it's the Cotswolds, everything's organic, locally sourced, and served in biodegradable packaging. Even the burgers feel like they've been on a yoga retreat before hitting the grill.

And for the hardcore Feastival fans, you can camp there. That's right—you can pitch a tent and wake up in the middle of a field, surrounded by the smell of fresh pastries and a vague hangover. They've even got "glamping" options for people who like the idea of camping but don't want to deal with things like damp grass or putting up a tent. So you can enjoy your morning espresso and croissant in a bell tent, pretending you're Bear Grylls but with better shoes.

Of course, there are loads of things for the kids too. Face painting, crafts, climbing walls—it's basically an outdoor crèche with better snacks. This means you can ditch the little ones for an hour and head off to sip prosecco while listening to a band you loved in the 90s. That's the magic of The Big Feastival: it lets you be a responsible adult and a slightly tipsy teenager all in the same day.

In the end, The Big Feastival isn't just an event—it's a state of mind. It's where music meets food, where camping meets comfort, and where Alex James proves that you can go from rock star to cheese star without missing a beat. It's not just a festival; it's the Cotswolds having the time of its life.

The Big Feastival: Bank Holiday August weekend (Fri-Sun). www.thebigfeastival.com.

57 LONGBOROUGH FESTIVAL OPERA

Longborough Festival Opera is like opera, but with a countryside twist, as if Puccini decided to swap Milan for a pair of wellies. It's held in a lovely village in the Cotswolds, which is basically where rich people go to pretend they're farmers. Longborough itself is so small you'd miss it if you blinked, but somehow, it hosts this world-class opera festival every summer. It's proof that you can put anything anywhere in the Cotswolds and make it posh.

The opera takes place in this theatre that's basically someone's big shed—well, technically a barn. But it's not just any barn; it's a fancy barn, converted with seats and acoustics so perfect that even cows would appreciate it if they got in. It's intimate, which is a polite way of saying "quite small," so you're really up close and personal with the singers. It's like karaoke but for people who actually know what they're doing.

Now, opera itself is a bit like singing but more serious. Instead of just singing about falling in love, they sing about falling in love while dying of tuberculosis or being stabbed or something else tragic. At Longborough, they're especially good at Wagner, who wrote operas that go on for so long you might need to bring a packed lunch. People come from all over the world to see Wagner here, because apparently, sitting in a barn in Gloucestershire for five hours is the height of sophistication.

The audience is what makes it really special. You get people in evening wear sipping champagne on picnic blankets, like they're at a very classy garden party. They bring hampers full of smoked salmon and quiche, which is a bit weird because there's also a bar and food stalls. But no, they insist on showing off their Waitrose-level picnic game. It's not just opera—it's competitive dining.

Of course, there's always a chance it might rain, because this is Britain. But even then, people just pull out their umbrellas and carry on as if sitting in a damp field listening to people sing in German is perfectly normal. That's the British spirit for you: wet but determined.

In summary, Longborough Festival Opera is like Glastonbury for people who'd rather hear a soprano than a guitar solo. It's posh, it's rural, and it's full of drama—both on and off the stage. If you've ever wanted to hear someone sing their heart out about betrayal while you nibble on a scotch egg, this is the place for you.

Longborough Festival Opera: New Banks Fee, Longborough, Moreton in Marsh, Glocs, GL56 0QF. www.lfo.org.uk

58 PUBS IN THE COTSWOLDS

Pubs in the Cotswolds are like drinking in a postcard—charming, historic, and probably hiding a few ghosts in the cellar. They've perfected the art of being old-fashioned but posh, serving you beer in places where you'd half expect to see a knight walk in and order a pint of mead. There are literally hundreds of amazing pubs dotted throughout this part of England. Most were built in the 16th century as stopping places for tired horses and weary travellers. You won't have to travel far or search very hard to find a great Cotswold pub. But if you want the absolute pinnacle of this Cotswoldy perfection, there's really only one place to go: the Horse & Groom Inn at Upper Oddington (shameless plug!).

This pub is so quintessentially Cotswolds it might as well come with its own herd of sheep. From the outside, it's a honey-colored stone building that looks like it was built for a BBC period drama. Inside, it's even better: a roaring fire, beams older than some countries, and usually more dogs than people. Seriously, there are dogs everywhere. It's like a canine convention where humans are allowed to join if they buy the drinks and treats. There is a wall dedicated to photographs of regulars' dogs and dogs even get their own menu!

Speaking of drinks, the Horse & Groom is famous for its ales, which are so good they've been scoring 100% with Cask Marque for years. These are proper ales, the kind that make you feel slightly smug drinking them, even if you don't really know what "hoppy" means. Ales so authentic that they will turn you into the beardy type you've always dreamed of being, and that's just the ladies. The pub also serves fantastic wines and spirits for when you're in the mood to be fancy.

The hospitality here is next level. The staff greet you like an old friend, even if it's your first visit. You'll get the sense they're genuinely thrilled you're here, which is rare for British service. It's the sort of place where they remember your dog's name before they remember yours—and that's exactly how it should be.

But the real star of the show? The food. The Horse & Groom is famous for its steaks and seafood, which are so good they should come with their own awards ceremony. The steaks are cooked to perfection—juicy, flavorful, and big enough to make you wonder if they were carved from some mythical beast. And the seafood? You'd think you were dining by the coast, not in the middle of the Cotswolds. It's fresh, expertly prepared, and genuinely unforgettable.

So, while the Cotswolds is full of charming pubs, the Horse & Groom Inn at Upper Oddington isn't just a pub—it's *the* pub.

Great ales, incredible food, relaxed hospitality, and more wagging tails than you can count. It's not just a place to eat and drink; it's a destination, an experience, and quite possibly the closest you'll get to perfection in pint form.

Horse and Groom Inn: Upper Oddington, Moreton in Marsh, Gloucestershire, GL56 0XH. www.horseandgroomcotswolds.co.uk. T: +44 (0)1451 830584.

INDEX

ABOUT THE AUTHOR

Warren Turner is landlord of the Horse and Groom Inn at Upper Oddington. He has owned the pub with his partner, Norman Liu, since March 2019. Prior to owning the pub, he worked as a professor in health and social care in London and has worked in higher education in New Zealand, Australia, Ukraine and Russia. He has authored and edited other books, but you probably won't want to read those as they are medical textbooks and contain a lot of gory details and pictures of medical conditions that might just cause you to have nightmares. Best stick to this one then, at least for now… He and Norman live in the Cotswolds with their two dogs. When they aren't behind the bar at the pub they can often be found propping up the bar of someone else's.